"Hello?"

"Gennifer?"

"Yes."

"Hi. It's Bill Clinton."

Sleeping
with the
President

A personal message from the publisher of Anonymous Press, Carson City, Nevada—

"History is written by those who prevail."

This book is dedicated to my parents, family, and friends, without whose love and support I would not have survived.

To the people at Anonymous Press, who had the belief, determination, and courage to make this book a tremendous success. To Jamie Forbes, a very insightful, professional, and talented man, without whose expertise this project would never have been possible.

To all the "other women" in this world who have cried for me and with me . . . there is a light at the end of the tunnel—just go toward it.

—Gennifer Flowers

Sleeping with the President

My Intimate Years with Bill Clinton

◆

Gennifer Flowers

Anonymous Press
Carson City • New York

Contents

Chapter 1. Bill Clinton Undressed   1

Chapter 2. What Did I Get Myself Into?   19

Chapter 3. Our First Date   31

Chapter 4. The Passion Begins   41

Chapter 5. Momma's Boy and Lover Man   51

Chapter 6. A Dream That Could Never Come True   63

Chapter 7. Stolen Moments with Mr. Kinky   75

Chapter 8. Portrait of a Risk Junkie   87

Chapter 9. The Long Goodbye   101

Chapter 10. Living Proof   117

References   131

Cast of Characters

Gennifer Flowers Singer and musician; former television journalist.

Bill Clinton President of the United States, former Governor of Arkansas, Rhodes scholar, and saxophone player.

Hillary Clinton First Lady and erstwhile attorney at one of Little Rock's esteemed law firms.

Edmund G. (Jerry) Brown, Jr. Former Governor of California and Bill Clinton's most savage (and pompous) rival for the 1992 Democratic Presidential nomination.

Dale Bumpers United States Senator from Arkansas and noted wit; formerly Arkansas State Senator.

George Bush Former President of the United States, Vice President under Ronald Reagan; beloved former director of the Central Intelligence Agency, venture-capitalist oilman, and celebrated member of Yale's Skull-and-Bones society.

Jimmy and **Rosalynn Carter** Former President and First Lady of the United States. Jimmy is an eminent international diplomatic troubleshooter, esteemed humanitarian, and well-regarded poet; he was formerly Governor of Georgia and a major-league peanut broker.

Roy Clark Country & Western superstar.

Mario Cuomo   Former Governor of New York and one of the modern masters of public rhetoric.

Vincent Foster   White House counsel and former law partner of Hillary Clinton; Foster's death by gunshot gave rise to an arcane web of steamy political and personal speculation.

Judy Gaddy   Personal Assistant to Governor Bill Clinton; assisted Bill Clinton in getting Gennifer Flowers the state job.

Richard Gephardt   United States Representative from Missouri, noted raconteur, and respected Congressional power broker.

Al Gore   Vice President of the United States, former United States Senator from Tennessee, and best-selling author. Al is wed to the ebullient Tipper, self-styled public censor and would-be protector of the nation's youth.

Gary Johnson   Little Rock attorney and former neighbor of Gennifer Flowers at the Quapaw Tower Apartments; Johnson suffered severe bodily injury when it was alleged he possessed clandestine videotapes of Bill Clinton's visitations.

Larry Nichols   Arkansas State worker whose actions surrounding the loss of his job involved the unearthing of several statewide scandals.

Finis Shellnutt   Internationally respected investment broker.

Chapter 1

♦

Bill Clinton Undressed

"Even the President of the United States sometimes must have to stand naked."

—Bob Dylan

Sleeping with the President is an intimate account of my twelve-year love affair with Bill Clinton and its continuing aftermath. I believe that you should not read this book unless you want to:

- Feel the passion as Bill Clinton and I spend our first lustful hours together—and begin a torrid love affair that lasts for more than a decade.
- Discover the president's candid feelings about his unhappy marriage, and listen to his comments about a variety of public figures.
- Follow Bill Clinton as he constantly takes bold, and sometimes foolish, risks to pursue his ravenous and kinky sexual desires.
- Unravel the hidden personal mysteries that conceal an unscrupulous president who expertly hides behind a carefully crafted public persona.
- Draw your own conclusions about what Bill Clinton's insatiable lust for women and power says about his fitness to be president.

◆

There are a lot of sexy and funny parts to the Gennifer Flowers–
Bill Clinton story. There are also some important lessons to be
learned, both about the way we lead our lives and the way politics is
conducted in America.

Some of you may ask: Is it right to take the intimate details of a
hot romance and stick them right in the face of the public? Can
disclosing such revelations be justified when the fate of our country
may be hanging in the balance?

I believe the answer to both questions is yes, and I'll tell
you why.

I have always considered my sex life to be private business, but
my erotic stolen moments with our forty-second president is an
entirely different matter. I know in my heart that I am *the* signifi-
cant other woman in the president's life. Beyond that, I sincerely
believe that I am the great love of his life.

Perhaps you'll recall an exchange of dialogue that took place on
60 Minutes shortly after news of my affair with Bill hit the national
media. It was Super Bowl Sunday, and the Clintons had decided to
go on TV to prove to the public that theirs was a loving marriage.

Bill would not admit that he had an affair—much less reveal
that I was his lover. All he was willing to say was that he and Hillary
had some marital difficulties, which were now behind them. It was
then that the interviewer, Steve Kroft, pointedly said:

"I think most Americans would agree that it's very admirable
that you . . . have stayed together, that you've worked your problems
out, that you seem to have reached some sort of an understanding
and an arrangement."

Bill Clinton did not appreciate that characterization, as you can
see by his response:

"Wait a minute," the future president objected. "You're looking
at two people who love each other. This is not an arrangement or an
understanding. This is a marriage. That's a very different thing."

It's a good thing Bill didn't have the same dilemma as Pinocchio.

If he had, millions of Americans would have seen his nose come right through their TV screens.

It is now common knowledge that Bill's relationship with Hillary is nothing more than an arrangement between two partners in power. Of course, I knew this was the case soon after I met Bill, but so did many other people who were part of the Little Rock scene in those days.

As revelations of Bill's womanizing continue to surface, I become ever more certain he has never gotten over me. And though it's doubtful we will ever embrace again, I guess I haven't completely gotten over him either.

I have had a number of serious monogamous relationships since Bill, but none has ultimately worked out. Maybe it's just that the right guy hasn't yet come along. Frankly, I'm beginning to wonder if he ever will.

So now you may be asking yourself, "How naive can Gennifer Flowers be? If her ex-lover is screwing dozens—perhaps even hundreds—of other women, isn't that a sure sign that he no longer gives a hoot about her?"

I surely can't fault you for seeing it that way. Still, in my heart, I feel we have the kind of connection that can only be shared by true soulmates.

I sometimes have dreams of Bill and me; we're floating in separate parts of an infinite sky—looking for that emotional resting place neither of us will ever find. Once, we touched each other in places shared only by the most deeply passionate lovers. But, apparently, we were never destined to wind up together—at least not in this life.

This reality saddens me, but I've learned to live with it. I continue to pursue meaningful relationships, in hope that some day I can find a soulmate who is also a lifemate. When I start getting down on myself for holding on too tightly to the past, I sometimes find consolation in the soothing words of Thomas Moore:

◆

If our dreams keep us attached to people we'd rather let go, then we could take the lead of these dreams and ease up on our spirited desire for change, giving a place to our sometimes painful and disturbing memories. If we singlemindedly [try to deny] . . . these attachments, then we are in danger of losing a degree of soulfulness. Liberation acquired at the cost of soul's desire can prove to be a questionable achievement.

I suppose I've always understood that Bill's quest for political power was the strongest of all his considerable cravings, and I knew this would one day tear us apart. Still, rational understanding is never the driving force when you're madly in love.

I truly loved this man and wanted to be with him as much as I possibly could. It was that simple. There is no question Bill had similar feelings toward me, but his life was far more complicated than mine—and not just because he was already married. We both started out with a lot of ambition, but I always had limits on how far I would go to achieve mine. That turned out not to be the case with Bill.

As you will see, Bill Clinton is a man with voracious appetites. The man loves food and he loves sex—but it has long been clear that he would have been glad to trade a lifetime of juicy sex and succulent steaks to be President of the United States for a single day.

Now Bill has achieved the presidency, thanks in no small measure to a wife who is every bit as power hungry as her man. At the same time, there is a mound of evidence that he has continued his brazen pursuit of other women—even that he sneaks out of the White House for late-night trysts.

Hillary Rodham Clinton is far too smart a lady to be fooled. Let's face it, she'd have to be a moron not to know she's married to a philanderer. Hillary certainly knew about me, and I'm sure she still has ways of keeping tabs on old Billy boy. Then again, our commander in chief has never been big on discretion.

There have been many prominent first ladies, but none with the stones to seize the reins of power as brazenly as Hillary has. I sometimes find myself thinking: "Who the hell elected her president?"

For better or worse, Hillary Rodham is the woman Bill chose to be his helpmate. And, like most other aspects of his rise to power, it was a carefully calculated choice. Even before he went off to college, Bill told his family he would never marry a beauty queen. He intended to marry the smartest girl in the class.

"You have to remember," an old Arkansas friend recalled, "that Billy grew up where women who dressed flossy and used a lot of cosmetics were 'available.' He wasn't ever going to *marry* that kind."

Men have often described me as a pretty girl with big breasts, so I realized I was more the "beauty queen" than the "class brain" in Bill's eyes. But Bill also gave me credit for being a smart, ambitious career woman with whom he could speak seriously—and we often did have wide-ranging discussions that went on for hours on end.

Did Bill see me as potential first lady material? I don't have the answer to that. He often talked dreamily about a time in the future when the two of us could really be together, but he probably never gave serious thought to leaving a wife who had quickly positioned herself to have an indispensable role in his presidential ambitions.

Despite his apparent success, I sense a desperate hunger in Bill's actions. The man has demonstrated he's a compulsive womanizer who will lie to cover his tracks, yet he is still tremendously popular with a good number of Americans.

It's interesting to look at some of the things prominent people were saying when I went public with my tape-recorded conversations with Bill. Take this interchange on *Donahue* between that former talk show host and Larry Sabato, a college professor and author of *Feeding Frenzy: How Attack Journalism Has Transformed American Politics.*

The panelists were debating whether it was appropriate to report allegations of a presidential candidate's marital infidelities. After admitting that the line was fuzzy, Phil Donahue asked Larry

Sabato where that line should be drawn. What he said was, "How many women does a guy have to cheat with before the press should report it?"

Larry Sabato answered the question this way: "The line ought to be drawn where the private behavior directly and seriously affects public performance. In the case of sexual liaisons, where it's compulsive behavior, where it's reckless behavior. . . .Where it's manifestly indiscreet."

It seems to me that Bill Clinton has more than satisfied those negative criteria both before and during his presidency. On the surface, any and all allegations of wrongdoing seem to roll right off Bill—who has become a living testament to that old adage that you never admit wrongdoing no matter how great the evidence against you.

When people like Bill are caught with their various appendages in the proverbial cookie jar, they either shuck and jive as he and Hillary did on *60 Minutes*, or they simply ask: "Who are you going to believe, me or your lying eyes?"

Every time allegations of wrongdoing come up, they are portrayed by the Clinton spin doctors as part of a sinister conspiracy to defeat the Forces of Good. That kind of hypocrisy is one of the main reasons I refuse to fade into the woodwork.

I know Bill Clinton intimately—and I am not just speaking in the biblical sense. I have firsthand knowledge of who the man is, and I feel it's my obligation to share that knowledge with the American people.

There have been all sorts of scandals that have cast a shadow over the Clinton presidency, and more evidence of chicanery seems to surface with each passing day. There are those who think it inevitable that Bill, Hillary, or both will eventually be indicted for some of their shenanigans.

If anything short of an indictment can bring down the president, it is his ongoing lack of veracity over his personal and political conduct. Whitewater will continue to dog the Clintons, as will

"Travelgate," "Filegate," and Vincent Foster's suicide. And there are some other long-standing credibility problems that keep coming up.

People who have served in the armed forces never fail to raise the president's alleged draft dodging whenever young soldiers are put in harm's way. Many with liberal leanings have not forgiven Clinton for backing out on his commitment to allow gays in the military. Then there was his lame "I never inhaled pot" pronouncement—one of many falsehoods of which I have firsthand knowledge.

With all this smoke, the President's nonstop adultery is the one so-called character issue that will continue to catch fire, because Bill Clinton will keep on sleeping with women other than his wife. And if he couldn't come clean about his affair with me, how can he ever be expected to admit that he has an uncontrollable sex drive?

The president's apologists keep trying to pass off each allegation of sexual misconduct as just more garbage to fill the tabloids. Surely they must know better.

Let's be honest. The details of Whitewater put most people to sleep—though few doubt the sleaziness of these dealings. And Filegate. Imagine the President of the United States hiring thugs to gather information on real or perceived adversaries. Am I wrong, or didn't we already have a president who was fond of compiling enemies lists?

It's relatively easy for the Clinton spin doctors to cloak such allegations in an ocean of legal gibberish—which is exactly what they've done. But brazenly cheating on your wife and then lying about it is a horse of a different color. Everyone knows what that's all about, and can relate to it on a gut level.

Is it sexy and fun to hear about a president's peccadilloes? I would expect so. But should it affect his political destiny? That is a question each of us needs to consider seriousl. Here again, I come back to what Professor Larry Sabato said on *Donahue*:

"Character is important in judging candidates. But why is it that we can only judge character based on bedroom behavior? Why can't we focus on other public aspects that reveal character, like how they treat their staffs, like what their peers think of them, like the times they've stood up and taken courageous stands or the times they haven't stood up and taken courageous stands?"

As you read my story, you will see that I have no complaints about the way Bill treated me as a lover. Fact is, he was a wonderful and giving lover—one who was usually far more interested in giving pleasure than in maintaining control. It's in other areas where the man's character is wanting.

I would ask that you consider Bill Clinton's behavior as a totality and reflect upon what it says about his sense of integrity. Is this person qualified to hold the world's most powerful office? Based on his actions, Bill is not someone I want to be president, even if I still carry a torch for the guy.

Maybe if all this scandal hadn't exploded, we might have still had a chance. That's no longer in the cards. However much he may love me, Bill could never forgive what he must feel are inexcusable acts of betrayal on my part. In any case, I have no regrets about coming forward. As much as I love him, Bill's actions reveal him to be a man of very questionable virtue.

Bill Clinton lied to me when he said I was his only lover. Apparently he was having sex with other women during our affair. More importantly, he left me hanging out to dry after convincing me to deny we were lovers in order to save his troubled candidacy.

People have asked why I want to expose myself to public scrutiny once again. Even though several versions of the Gennifer Flowers story have been out there, I have never before told the whole, uncensored version of my affair with Bill Clinton and its ramifications on both our lives. With this book, I finally have the editorial freedom and the emotional perspective to do just that.

I continue to be attacked by much of the mainstream media who are more interested in backing a particular horse than reporting the truth. I am tired of being referred to as Clinton's "alleged" mistress, though I no longer let such insults anger or depress me. My relationship with the president has been well established, despite the lack of what some journalists call "a smoking gun."

Hell, what was I supposed to do to validate my story? Hire a private investigator to take photos of us in bed? I'm just not that kind of person. In fact, the only people I know who do things like that are gangsters and power-hungry politicians. Whenever this issue comes up, it makes me think of the words the Michael Corleone character used in *The Godfather* to defend his father's unconventional ways:

"My father is a businessman trying to provide for his wife and children and those friends he might need someday in a time of trouble. He doesn't accept the rules of the society we live in because those rules would have condemned him to a life not suitable for a man like himself, a man of extraordinary force and character. . . . He considers himself the equal of all great men like Presidents and Prime Ministers and Supreme Court Justices and Governors of the States. He refuses to live by rules set up by others. . . . But his ultimate aim is to enter that society with a certain power since society doesn't really protect its members who do not have their own individual power. In the meantime he operates on a code of ethics he considers far superior to the legal structures of society."

Perhaps it's true that real organized-crime families have a fairer, more humane set of values than some of our politicians. It breaks my heart that Bill Clinton turns out to be a man I would compare unfavorably to a Mafia don. But maybe that's what it takes to be president of the United States these days. If that's actually true, we could well be doomed as a nation.

People still ask why I decided to go public with my story prior to the 1992 election. The answer is that I was pretty much forced into it. I was also in a position to back up my allegations with tape-recorded phone conversations—portions of which are reprinted in this book. Those taped conversations continue to speak volumes about Bill Clinton—however hard he and his spin meisters try to discredit them.

Yes, it's true that I was compensated for my story in several instances, but I never would have talked to the press had the story not been leaked beforehand. Even then, I would have continued to deny it, as Bill can be heard asking me to do on one of the tapes. But by this time, he had abandoned me. I felt vulnerable and scared— and for good reason.

My apartment had been illegally entered on three separate occasions, and my life was threatened. Worse still, they tried to intimidate my mother. Some man called her and without identifying himself said in gruff, muffled tones, "You should be real proud of your daughter. She'd be better off dead."

Understandably, my mother was worried sick about my safety. I was mortified that she had been dragged into this. At the time, Mom was living in a small town in Missouri. Not only that, she was remarried and was no longer using the name Flowers.

It was obvious that someone had gone to a lot of trouble to track down my family. They were trying to hit me where I was most easily hurt, and they had succeeded. "Oh, Bill," my heart cried out. "Could you really have been behind all this?" But in my mind, the answer was clear.

Over the years, I've seen what has happened to people who try to cross Bill Clinton. As in the case with Mafia dons, it is never the number-one man who directly makes threats, much less commits acts of violence. I envision these things going down very much like Mario Puzo described them in *The Godfather:*

> "Between the head of the family . . . who dictated policy and the men who actually carried out the orders of the Don, there were three layers, or buffers. In that way, nothing could be traced to the top. . . . Each link of the chain would have to turn traitor for the Don to be involved. Though it had never yet happened, there was always the possibility. The

cure for that possibility was also known. Only one link in the chain had to disappear."

This same kind of buffer system would make it almost impossible to find out for certain who was behind the threats to me and my family. Still, I've often asked myself: Who had something to gain by frightening me and my mother half to death?

If the culprit wasn't Bill Clinton himself, it was more than likely someone closely connected with him or his campaign. Perhaps all Bill did was say to an underling that someone had better figure a way to keep Gennifer quiet. No more than that had to be spoken to get the less-than-subtle message across: *Do whatever is necessary to get the job done. I don't need to be apprised of any specifics.*

There are those who will attribute my suspicions to sour grapes or an overactive imagination. But believe me, I know of what I speak.

Even before I had been threatened, I was aware of the harm that could come to people who crossed Bill Clinton or the power structure he represented. Word had it that the state troopers who worked for Bill had threatened and roughed up Bill's enemies. At least one of those incidents involved an attempt to cover up Bill's affair with me.

An attorney named Gary Johnson lived next door to me in the Quapaw Tower—the high-rise in Little Rock where I lived in the late 1980s, during the last stage of my affair with Bill. I didn't really know Gary Johnson, other than to say hello when we met in the hall. For reasons that still aren't completely clear to me, Gary placed a video camera in the hall in such a way that it produced a clear view of my apartment door.

When rumors began circulating that Bill and I were having an affair, Gary let it be known that he was in possession of a videotape of Bill coming to my apartment. Shortly thereafter, a couple of thugs forced their way into his place, beat Gary senseless and left him for dead. According to Gary, they kept asking him where "the tape" was. Gary eventually recovered from his wounds, but the videotape with Bill on it had disappeared from his apartment.

In another incident, a female cousin of Bill's accused a man I'll call Randolph of raping her. This gal had previously identified two other men, but both came up with alibis. Only then did she point the finger at Randolph.

There was never proof of vaginal rape, much less that Randolph was the culprit. Nevertheless, while Randolph was out on bail, the sheriff and the girl's father attacked him, cut off his testicles and left him for dead. Randolph's sons found him and got him to a hospital. Meanwhile, the sheriff put the severed testicles on display in his office.

Randolph sued his assailants in civil court and won, but was never paid any money. At the criminal trial, an expert witness was not allowed to testify that the semen found on the girl's clothes was not Randolph's. Consequently, Randolph was sent to prison for rape. As far as I know, he's still rotting away in some godforsaken Arkansas prison.

Now, I very much doubt that Bill Clinton gave any specific orders in either of these horrible assaults. But again I ask, whose interests were being served?

Please keep in mind that this is not just innuendo designed to discredit Bill Clinton. It's part of the public record. As the saying goes, you could look it up.

There are, of course, many other allegations of strong-arm tactics that have surfaced, especially those designed to prevent what one Clinton insider so delicately referred to as "bimbo eruptions." I may be the love of Bill's life, but I certainly wasn't the only "other woman" he slept with. Not by a long shot. Nor was I the only one of his ex-lovers who was the victim of intimidation.

A former Miss Arkansas, who apparently had an affair with Bill while I was living in Texas, told a British journalist that she was approached by a man named Tucker, who claimed he represented the Democratic party. Tucker said she would be given a federal job if she would not go public about her affair with the president.

"If I was a good little girl and [kept my mouth shut]," she told the journalist, "I'd be set for life: a federal job, nothing fancy, but a regular paycheck. . . . I'd never have to worry again."

The woman claims that Tucker then threatened her, saying that "they" knew she jogged by herself, and that he "couldn't guarantee what would happen to her pretty little legs."

The terrified woman declined Tucker's offer and was soon fired from her job. One of the woman's coworkers overheard her conversation with Tucker and reported the incident to the FBI. Sources at the Bureau will only say that there is an ongoing investigation into the matter.

Several weeks after her encounter with Mr. Tucker, the woman found a shotgun shell on the front seat of her Jeep and the car's back window shattered. She also received a threatening note that read, "I'll pray you have a head-on collision and end up in a coma. Marilyn Monroe got snuffed. It could happen."

As more women continue to come forward with allegations, my story has become increasingly problematic for Bill and his people. Unless someone manages to catch Bill in the act with another woman, I am the closest thing they have to a smoking gun.

Will the revelations in this book put me in harm's way once again? Maybe so. But, on some level, I have never really been out of danger. I continue to receive anonymous phone calls and veiled threats. But that's the price you pay for going against Bill Clinton.

One interesting twist to the stories of intimidation has to do with the same Arkansas state troopers. These are some of the same thugs Bill used to cover up his affairs and harass people. Since Bill has become president, several of those troopers have told their stories to, among other people, David Brock, who writes for the *American Spectator*.

I have no desire to rehash Bill Clinton's many adulterous

affairs and risky casual encounters as revealed by the troopers. What I am interested in are the bribes and threats that were employed to intimidate those same men that then-Governor Clinton used to extort others.

One of the troopers, Larry Patterson, claims that when I first made public my affair with Bill in 1992, my ex-lover was furious. "What does that whore think she's doing to me?" he reportedly shouted.

Patterson told David Brock that his boss, Buddy Young, who was then chief of security for Governor Clinton, was instructed to make certain that no other women came forward. Patterson told Brock that Young believed that if even one other ex-lover was allowed to tell her story, "Gennifer would be credible."

Young also warned the troopers in Clinton's security detail to keep their mouths shut: "If you're smart," he told them, "you won't talk to the press."

Young succeeded in keeping a lid on the tales of Bill Clinton's sexual exploits during the 1992 campaign, and his boss managed to win the election. For performing this essential service to his don, Buddy Young was rewarded with a $92,300-a-year federal job.

When he found out that Patterson and three other troopers were about to go public with their stories, Young again tried to intercede.

"I represent the president of the United States," he told trooper Roger Perry. "Why do you want to destroy him over this? You don't know anything anyway. . . . This is not a threat, but I wanted you to know that your own actions could bring about dire consequences."

Larry Patterson claims that Young sent him a handwritten note expressing concern for Patterson's health. When questioned by David Brock, Young admitted that he had been in contact with the three troopers to discuss this matter.

"I called Roger as a friend, and I told him I thought this was wrong, it was unethical, and it was a disgrace to security people. But I never said I spoke for the president, because I don't."

Young didn't deny sending a note to Patterson about his health, but insisted that the note was not meant as a veiled threat. "Larry has heart problems," Young told David Brock, "and I was concerned about his cholesterol."

I don't know whether to laugh or cry when I'm reminded that this was the man whose job it was to destroy my credibility. But, as time goes on, the public has come to realize that it is the veracity of Bill Clinton and his organized political "family" that really needs to be scrutinized.

It's not so much a question of whether the public should care about the sex lives of their leaders as much as the implicit corruption and potential dangers of having a president whose compulsive sexual needs are so out of control. As investigative journalist Roger Morris concludes in his book *Partners in Power:*

> It was not that Clinton had governed and then made his sexual forays as part of some scrupulously separate private life. In part because of the furtive shadow play with Hillary, in part the product of his own . . . sense of entitlement, much of the philandering took place during the workday on official trips or around ceremonial or political functions. He had indulged a good deal of his relentless promiscuity *as* the government. Propositioning young women at county fairs or enticing state employees at conferences, he enjoyed much of his predatory privilege because he *was* the government.
>
> There was also the issue of how much the illicit practices opened the governor and future president to blackmail or how much the gifts and other expenses which could not be taken from any legitimate income that Hillary might notice made him all the more dependent on his own "walking around" cash from backers. Equally telling was what it all revealed about his genuine attitude toward women. The repeated testimony of the troopers would show the

undisguised Clinton rating women as objects, "ripe peaches" as he called them, purely to be graded, purely to be chased, dominated, conquered.

When we were together, Bill always treated me with respect and consideration. He never forced himself upon me in any way, and made me feel that he regarded me as a friend as well as a lover. On the other hand, I can believe that he called me a whore after I went public with our affair. After all, I had betrayed him and, therefore, had become the enemy.

In spite of everything that has happened, I don't feel Bill is my enemy. I still care about him in many ways—though he certainly has shown that he doesn't possess many of the qualities I want in a president. When I first met Bill Clinton, however, he appeared to possess almost all the qualities I wanted in a lover. At the time, that was all I cared about. Who could have guessed where it would lead?

Chapter 2

♦

What Did I Get Myself Into?

"When people elect a president, they not only want a person who promotes good policies, but also someone on whom they can depend. They like to think they're electing a Lincolnesque figure—and not a Caligula of the Ozarks."

—Tony Snow, syndicated columnist

I'm standing in the middle of a large room, surrounded by screaming people. Multicolored spotlights are pointed at me. On the left, there are defenders of Bill Clinton, liberal media types, and members of NOW. They're all calling me "bimbo," and shaking their fists at me.

On the right, there are representatives of the Republican party, Dittoheads wearing Rush Limbaugh T-shirts, and pro-lifers. They don't seem as angry as the people on the left, but they're screaming just as loud—imploring me to join them in "nailing Slick Willie to the cross."

Mixed in throughout the crowd, there are dozens of high-pressure sales reps holding checkbooks. Some want me to put my name to untrue stories about my relationship with President Clinton. Others want to take nude photos of me. "Come with me, Gennifer," they shout. "I'll make you rich. I'll make you a star."

Everyone is hollering at the same time. They've all closed in on me. I'm being pulled at, smothered, crushed. I can't breathe. I'm screaming my head off, but I can't even hear myself.

Where am I? Please, get me out of this place!

Wait a second. All the noise seems to have quieted down, and
. . . I'm not even standing up. It's pitch black in here. Hey, what
happened to all those spotlights?

I rub my eyes. It's three A.M. and I'm lying in my bed. The whole
thing was a nightmare.

I'm relieved, but I can't get back to sleep. My mind keeps playing the same piece of film over and over again. And even though
I'm wide awake, I can still hear that deafening chorus of voices
barking at me. I try to talk myself through it.

Okay, Gennifer. Try to concentrate. You've got to listen beyond
those screaming voices to hear the whispers that come from your
heart. They're saying, "Forget about all the terrible things people
have said and done to you. Your love affair with Bill Clinton was
never meant to be about politics or money."

*That's true. Whatever else it has become, what Bill and I had was
mostly a romance—the most passionate romance of both our lives. It just so
happens that my lover was destined to become the forty-second president of
the United States. I can remember how it all started as clearly as if it were
yesterday. . . .*

I first met Bill Clinton on a fall evening in 1977. He was the
attorney general of Arkansas and I was a news reporter for television
station KARK, the NBC affiliate in Little Rock. Bill and Arkansas
Senator Dale Bumpers had just attended a meeting in Washington,
and I was assigned to interview the attorney general as he stepped
off a plane at the Little Rock airport.

As hot and sticky as it was out at that airport, I found myself
shivering from nervousness. Attorney General Clinton was known
to be a warm and friendly person who related well to the press. But
I had been with the TV station for only a few weeks, and this was my
first major assignment.

Nobody expected my simple debriefing to reveal anything sig-
nificant. Still, I was very much the rookie who desperately wanted to

hit a home run. As I stood there, trying to sort through my list of questions, there was no way I could have guessed that the next sixty seconds would start a chain of events that would forever alter the course of my life.

As Bill Clinton approached the group of reporters, everyone started calling out questions. Because of my experience as a singer, I had no problem making myself heard.

"Mr. Clinton," I bellowed, "can I get a statement from you?"

The attorney general turned toward me, obviously intending to give an account of his Washington trip. But before he could utter a word, our eyes met. Right then, I felt a jolt of electricity run through my body.

In retrospect, I realize that Bill and I were experiencing what some would call love—or at least lust—at first sight. But romance was the last thing on my mind at that juncture. I was there to do a job, and had every intention of acting cool and professional.

Not so with Bill. His baby blue eyes grew wide, and his mouth broke into a mischievous smile. Bill just looked me up and down and asked suggestively, "Where did they find you?"

"Oh, brother!" I thought to myself. "The last thing I need now is some horny politician coming on to me." As I've said, people have often pegged me as a pretty girl with big breasts. Which is fine, except that people tend to stereotype sexy-looking women as being stupid bimbos who lack both intelligence and talent.

When I met Bill Clinton, I was twenty-seven years old, and had known my share of men. But being an attractive, sexy woman can be a double-edged sword. On the one hand, it opens up a lot of doors. Then again, those doors too often lead to a bed you have no interest in sharing.

That night at the Little Rock airport, I wasn't interested in anything that would make it harder for me to concentrate on performing my job. Which is exactly the effect Bill's come-on was having, and I resented it.

"Just another lech trying to jump my bones," I remember think-ing to myself. At the same time, another part of me couldn't help but notice that my heart was aflutter. No matter. The job was my first priority.

I looked at Bill innocently, pretending not to understand the less-than-subtle message he was sending when he uttered those five fateful words, "Where did they find you?"

I heard myself answer, "Actually, I just started working for the station recently." Then, before Bill had a chance to utter another sound, I plunged right into my prepared list of questions.

Skilled politician that he is, Bill quickly gathered himself and responded in a serious way. But that slow, sexy smile never left his face. His glowing eyes locked in on mine, and it felt as if we were the only two people in the airport.

Bill answered every one of my questions with rational, intelli-gent words, but the rest of his being was speaking a language that had nothing to do with our respective jobs as reporter and attor-ney general.

A few minutes later, Bill jumped into a waiting car and left. I was totally drained. Now that I had done my job, I could start processing all the feelings and sensations that were going through my body.

I thought Bill's timing was totally inappropriate, but the chem-istry between us was too strong to be denied. Still, there's a big difference between feeling turned on by someone and acting on those feelings.

I had no plans of letting this brief flirtation go any further. But later that night I was lying in bed, fantasizing over Bill. He was as cute as a button, sexy—and dangerous. I found myself obsessing over those bedroom eyes and that sensual mouth!

"Wait a minute, Gennifer," I said out loud. "What could you be thinking? This guy is a public figure—and he's married! So do your-self a big favor; steer clear of Mr. Bill Clinton."

Obviously, I didn't do the greatest job of convincing myself to forget about Bill. Over the next few weeks and months, I sometimes found myself covering meetings and events at which he was present. It seemed as if he was constantly staring at me. People would turn to see who Bill was gaping at, but that never stopped him.

If Bill had been single, I wouldn't have thought twice about giving the boy a run for his money. But I knew that getting involved with a married man could lead to big trouble. Anyway, there were plenty of cute guys around who weren't carrying all that baggage, and I've never had a problem finding them.

From the first, people assumed that I was attracted to Bill Clinton because he was powerful. That was never the case. In 1977, when I met Bill, he was the thirty-one-year-old attorney general of Arkansas. To me that was no big deal. In fact, I never got the impression that he was very impressed with that position either.

In any case, my interest in Bill Clinton had nothing to do with his public standing, or even that people in Little Rock believed he would one day be governor—maybe even president. Still, I can honestly say that Bill's being a politician didn't impress me in the least. In fact, I've never been attracted to men because of their political clout.

At the time Bill and I met, I might have fallen for a show business celebrity or a powerful businessman in the entertainment world, because that kind of thing appealed to me. I had been a singer and band leader since I was eleven years old, and that is where my strongest career ambitions were.

Over the years, I've been involved with a number of famous men, including Evel Knievel; comedian Rich Little; and rodeo champion Larry Mahan, who once caused a scene by lying down in the lobby of the Fairmont Hotel in Dallas until I agreed to go out with him. Entertainers might be screwballs in their way, but politicians never did hold much appeal for me as lovers—even fabulously wealthy ones.

My family was quite comfortable when I was growing up, and Daddy was active in Republican politics. When Winthrop Rockefeller ran for governor on the Republican ticket, my father was one of his staunchest supporters. Daddy was an airplane pilot, who owned several airports in Arkansas. Winthrop Rockefeller kept some of his planes at those airports, and Daddy knew him quite well.

Winthrop Rockefeller owned Petit Jean Mountain, where his house was located. Daddy would sometimes go to Petit Jean for special parties, most of them politically oriented. Being a Republican in a small Arkansas town was really bucking the system, since Democrats generally had an iron-clad lock on state and local politics.

Democratic governor Orval Faubus had been governor for twelve years, and Daddy was determined to help Rockefeller replace him. I was still in high school at the time, but I'd caught the bug from Daddy and eventually became president of the Young Arkansans for Rockefeller.

Arkansas was one of the poorest, most backward states in the country. It seemed to me that drastic changes were needed. We held mock elections in our high school and provided whatever assistance we could to the Rockefeller campaign. In the course of working for that campaign, I wound up meeting Winthrop Rockefeller, Jr. and he started asking me out.

My mother was thrilled that Winnie was interested in me. She was enamored with the idea that I would marry someone with the wealth and power of a Rockefeller. At one point, Winnie telephoned me from England. That impressed me, because I had never been pursued by a boy at such long distance.

Mother was ecstatic. She kept insisting, "You are going to go out with him. You are going to like him."

I did go out with Winnie a few times—mostly to appease my Mom. But I already had a boyfriend named Joe Clifton and didn't want to date anyone else.

I guess it's only natural for a mother to want her daughter to better herself, and I don't fault Mother for trying. Still, I couldn't see what the big deal was. I knew we weren't the Rockefellers, but it seemed to me that we had all the comforts a person could ever want. I lived in a nice home; drove a nice car; wore nice clothes. What else did I need?

At that time, I had no concept of what millions or billions of dollars were all about—but I have no regrets. Living a materially comfortable life is still important to me, but I'll take love over money or power any day of the week. That's exactly how I felt back in 1977. Anyhow, Bill didn't have very much money, and his position wasn't all that prestigious.

At the time Bill and I met, I was both a nightclub singer and a television reporter. In a provincial capital like Little Rock, that made me a celebrity in my own right. In addition, I was an attractive young woman who'd already fried much bigger fish than this married attorney general.

There had been plenty of opportunities to go out with politicians who were far more powerful than Bill Clinton—if that's what I'd been looking for. And unlike Bill, some of them were single and marriage material. But power and money were never what my relationship with Bill was about.

I was flattered by Bill's obvious interest in me, but I was also embarrassed by his lack of subtlety. Bill just laughed it off. It seemed like he couldn't care less if people knew that he was openly displaying his lust for someone other than his wife of eighteen months.

Everybody has since learned that coming on to women in public is Bill Clinton's modus operandi. At the time, I found his unabashed display of attention to be more refreshing than reckless.

I initially responded to Bill's seductive looks by flashing my "Do you mind?" glare. Then I'd turn away. That tactic didn't faze him; he just kept right on staring at me. People in the press corps and all over the capital had started whispering about us. There were already rumors that we were having an affair, though all that was happening at that point was a lot of overheated eye contact on his part.

I started thinking to myself, "What the hell; this could be fun."

I started returning Bill's lustful stares, which probably was the clincher in his mind.

Whenever we met, the two of us played an intense game of psychological foreplay. The vibes were getting hotter than the sweltering summer weather in Arkansas. Bill knew he'd captured my interest, but the obvious complications were never too far from my mind.

I remember the day Bill finally approached me. I was at the Justice Building covering a public service hearing about the rate increase for pay telephones. I was sitting up in the gallery area with the other reporters, and Bill was down on the floor. There were a number of things going on that day.

A woman who worked in the attorney general's office was handling the hearing for the most part. She was a young, heavyset woman in her twenties, and she was wearing out the opposition with her smart and feisty presentation.

I was turned on by the way this woman was doing her job, and I could see that Bill was enjoying it too. I later found out that one side of Bill loves women who are independent and smart enough to hold their own with men. That's exactly what this woman was doing—and then some.

After a while, Bill recognized that this gal was handling the hearing so well that he really didn't have to pay close attention to the proceedings. That's when he started getting into some heavy-duty eye contact.

By now, I had started becoming disillusioned with my job as a TV reporter, and I wasn't at all sure I wanted to continue doing that kind of work. Getting ahead in the TV news business was very difficult for a woman at that time. It was another one of those deals where being good looking turned out to be a double-edged sword.

TV stations had learned that attractive female reporters boosted their ratings, and I'm sure that helped me get hired. The problem is that the people around you tend to assume that you're there as a prop rather than as a professional.

If she's so good looking, the thinking goes, how could she possibly have any brains or insight or ability? I was committed to doing a good job, and felt like the work was going well. But I soon grew tired of the chauvinism and double standard that existed in that world.

After a few months, I simply didn't feel the same sense of responsibility toward my job as when I first started out. So, when Bill started wooing me with his eyes that particular day, I decided to return the favor in spades.

After a few minutes of heavy flirting, Bill suddenly disappeared from the floor. I guess he must have gone to his office. Eventually, I moved to the lobby area of the building, and was sitting there writing my lines. My cameraman was just outside, waiting for my signal to begin rolling the tape.

Just then, Bill came walking through the lobby, caught sight of me, and strutted right over. Without hesitation, he whispered, "I don't know about you, but I can't stand this anymore. I just have to see you. Would you give me your phone number?"

Even though this was anything but unexpected, I panicked. My cameraman could have walked through the door at any moment, and I didn't want him or anyone else to overhear us.

One part of me was glad Bill had finally asked, because I was feeling tremendously attracted to him. But, as much as I wanted him, I still couldn't stop thinking about all those complications.

What the hell? I decided to give him my number. But, in my mind, I still wasn't committed to seeing him. I figured I could always blow him off or not take his calls. Oh, well—I never was very good at deceiving myself. Anyhow, I quickly tore a page from my notebook, scribbled down my home number, and handed it to him.

It can be argued that I never should have even entertained the thought of dating a married man—much less winding up sleeping with him. But does submitting to that kind of temptation make me a tramp or a bimbo? I don't see it that way.

Remember, we're talking about the 1970s, and there was still a tremendous sense of sexual freedom in that environment. And let's face it: I wasn't exactly a prude or a virgin. But, apparently, I'm going to need several lifetimes to put up the kind of numbers our commander in chief has achieved.

Anyhow, when I gave Bill my phone number, I'm not sure what I envisioned. I certainly wasn't taking my emotional or physical security into consideration. So what was I thinking about? A roll in the hay? A torrid love affair? Frankly, I'm still not sure. I certainly never imagined, however, that my fate would forever be so intertwined with his.

Chapter 3

♦

Our First Date

"I loved being with her, but I had very ambivalent feelings about getting involved with her. I could just look at her and tell she was interesting and deep."

—Bill Clinton

J ust one day after I'd given Bill my telephone number, I had come home from work and was relaxing in my apartment when the phone rang.

"Hi, Gennifer," the voice on the other end of the line rasped. "If it's not inconvenient, I'd really like to stop by around eight-thirty."

Part of me still wanted to say no, but by then, it wasn't a very big part. Despite the potential pitfalls, I couldn't remember ever meeting a guy who was so charming and sexy. There was no other man of importance in my life at the time. So I let the urge get the best of me.

In most instances, I try to avoid first dates in my apartment, but this was a different situation. I knew that Bill and I couldn't meet out in public, so I agreed to let him come over.

That night, as I waited for Bill to arrive, I was nervous as a cat. There was a ballad playing on the radio, but I was much too fidgety to sit there and listen. Finally, I stood up and started pacing back and forth in my tiny living room.

I glanced over at the clock. It was 8:33. Maybe he had changed his mind, and decided to chuck the whole thing. Suddenly the doorbell rang, and I jumped up. I hesitated before opening the door.

A little voice inside me said, "Pull yourself together, girl." I took a deep breath, then unlatched the door.

There Bill stood with that charming smile, as his probing blue eyes locked onto mine. I was turned on physically, but apprehensive emotionally. Bill sensed my tension and, in no time at all, he put me at ease. His manner was relaxed and casual. I knew that he desperately wanted to make love, but did not yet know what he intended to do about it.

We sat down opposite one another at a table in my tiny living room on these two antique maplewood chairs. I uncorked a bottle of red wine and poured two glasses. Then we started talking.

Bill and I were sitting just inches from each other, and we could feel the sparks. Beyond that, we quickly connected as human beings. Bill started talking about how hard it was to get things done on his job. I was extremely interested in what he had to say, but I couldn't keep my eyes off his sensuous mouth.

For some reason, men's lips often aren't as full as those of women. A lot of guys have chicken lips. Some appear to have no lips at all. Not so with Bill. His lips are kind of full—especially his bottom lip. I really liked the way that bottom lip kind of turned to the side as he spoke.

We talked for hours, and he seemed genuinely interested in my opinions, which made me feel really special. This wasn't just about getting laid. The guy actually liked me.

Bill and I quickly discovered that we both had similar senses of humor, and the warm laughter that resounded through the room helped me feel completely relaxed. I realized that Bill wasn't going to make any sudden moves on me—which made him that much more desirable.

Bill would occasionally reach across the table and gently hold my hand and rub it a little. Whenever he wanted to make a particular point about something, he would let go of my hand and softly brush my leg. None of this was meant as a come-on. It was Bill demonstrating his passion for whatever subject we happened to be discussing. Everything about this interaction felt very natural.

Each time we touched, I could feel sparks of electricity going up and down my spine. By then I knew that we weren't going to consummate our erotic feelings that night, which made it even more enticing. I still get flush when I recall the warmth of that evening. I felt as if I had known Bill all my life.

I wasn't ready to call it love, but I liked Bill a lot. He was an intelligent, good-looking, passionate man who seemed interested in me as a person. His apparent desire to get to know *me*, rather than what was underneath my clothes, really made me feel good about him.

We talked about everything—politics, music, and what each of us was trying to accomplish in our careers. Bill confided that he planned to run for governor of Arkansas in the next election. Eventually he hoped that would lead to becoming president of the United States. I talked about my accomplishments in the entertainment business, as well as some of my frustrations.

"You and I are so much alike," Bill said at one point. And we were a lot alike.

It makes for an intriguing picture: Two people sitting in a tiny living room on a first date, talking about their dreams for the future. The small-town nightclub singer reveals that she plans to be a major recording artist. The local politician talks about becoming president of the United States.

If you think about it objectively, such dreams sound like foolishness. But instead of laughing in each other's face and saying, "That's a nice dream, but no way is it ever going to happen," the two people listen attentively and take each other seriously.

"There's no question in my mind that you could be president someday," I tell Bill.

"And I'm certain that, if you keep on pluggin'," Bill tells me, "you're gonna make it to the top of your business."

The great thing about our interaction was that we weren't patronizing one another or trying to score points with flattery.

At the time, I hadn't met too many men who had that kind of positive—some might say liberated—attitude. Most guys really didn't want to hear about a woman's career. A few claimed to like independent women who had strong professional goals. But many of them eventually became intimidated by the idea that they might have to take a backseat to a woman's career.

Over the years, I had dealt with a great deal of that kind of backward thinking, so Bill's support and encouragement was a refreshing change. Slowly, the thought started to gel in my mind.

This guy was the whole package: He's sexy, funny, and intelligent. Moreover, he seems to understand what I'm about, and he's not even trying to take off my clothes. As if all that wasn't enough, he reminded me of my father.

My daddy, Gene Flowers, had died in a plane crash in 1973, and I'd been devastated. Daddy was the only man who had ever loved me unconditionally. His death hit me hard, and I had difficulty shutting out the excruciating pain.

When I met Bill, I still hadn't fully gotten over the loss of my father. The similarity between the two men was almost eerie. Looking back, I realize that was probably a big part of what made Bill such a tremendous sexual and emotional turn-on. It also should have been a red flag that there was danger and heartbreak lurking around the corner.

Daddy was an incurable womanizer, and his philandering had caused my mother a great deal of pain. Mother was a strong and self-confident person, but she always felt insecure about Daddy. She loved him, but could never come to terms with his running around. Mother always wanted me on her side, and often used me as a pawn in her battles with Daddy.

I adored my father, but I also resented him for what he was

doing to our family. Eventually my folks divorced, and I was left with a great deal of anger toward my father.

As I've matured, I've come to understand my father as a complete person. I still don't condone his womanizing and its role in breaking up our home, but I'll always love him just the same.

As is the case with so many daughters and fathers, I never had a chance to sit down and tell Daddy how much he meant to me. Shortly before he died, we had started to heal some of the old wounds, but there was still a lot we needed to talk about. Suddenly, I had lost him forever. Some of those scars were still quite raw when I met Bill.

I came to realize that Daddy really did love my mother. Unfortunately, he had a weakness for other women. It didn't help that members of the opposite sex were attracted to my father's moviestar good looks and his reckless nature. I had heard that Bill also had a wife whom he respected, and a wandering eye that sometimes caused him to act recklessly.

As I sat in that kitchen, face-to-face with this new man in my life, I couldn't help wondering if Bill wasn't some kind of reincarnation of my father. Was I pushing the comparison too far? Maybe so. Still, there were so many similarities between the two men.

Like Bill, Daddy was a kind, gentle person, but he had his dark side. If somebody pushed Daddy, he wouldn't hesitate to throw a punch. Bill also had a temper, but he vented it in different ways. If you crossed Bill Clinton, he always made it a point to get even.

Who was it that I was really looking at across those glasses of red wine? Was it Bill Clinton or was it my daddy, Gene Flowers? For a moment there, the two men were indistinguishable in my mind. Maybe it was just the wine, though it sure seemed like there was something else going on.

Daddy had always been such a strong figure in my life. I'd never met another man who had been able to provide the kind of spark and emotional support he gave me. Was Bill that man? He certainly had that same sexy, come-hither look in his eyes, that same easygoing way about him that conveyed both a sense of danger and a feeling that said, "Don't worry, baby. Everything's gonna be all right!"

By now, the hour was getting late, and I didn't want the evening to end. Still, I had to get to work early to do the morning weather for the TV station, so I'd soon have to ask Bill to leave. I felt really good about the way things had gone. I was also very turned on by the anticipation of many nights together yet to come.

I have to say that this was anything but a typical Gennifer Flowers date back in 1977. At that time in my life, I was looking for adventure—not love. I was focused in on my career, and had never fantasized about a traditional marriage and living in a house with a white picket fence.

Back then, if I was on a first date with a man I was attracted to, we would almost always make love. That's just the way it was during that sexually liberated time.

I didn't know it then, but it turns out that Bill had sex with a number of women after his marriage to Hillary. Some have claimed that he groped them against their will. If that's true, they must be talking about someone other than the man who became my lover for twelve years. In any case, none of these women have ever described Bill as a man who holds back on his sexual impulses.

So what made this night different? From my vantage point, it had nothing to do with my reservations about Bill's being a married man. And if Bill really is the kind of hit-and-run lover some have described, there should have been nothing holding him back.

I believe the reason we didn't have sex that night is that it became evident shortly after Bill arrived that something special was going on between us. It was as if we both wanted to acknowledge that what we felt was about something a lot more important than just getting laid.

I can't recall ever feeling the need to delay fulfilling my sexual desires unless there was a very good reason. I certainly wasn't going to deprive myself of pleasure just because I wanted something deeper to take root.

Now, for the first time in my life, I was feeling rumbles of love. Sure, I had experienced some hot-and-heavy relationships when I was younger, as well as my share of casual sex. But I felt something different on that first date with Bill. It was as close as I'd ever come to a real, womanly love. Now that glorious night was about to come to an end.

"I could talk to you forever, Bill, but I really do have to get up bright and early," I said.

"Sure," he replied with a warm smile. "I understand. Anyway, it's late. I should be going too."

We both got up and walked to the door. Then Bill turned and put his lips on mine. His kiss was sweet and gentle—not passionate.

My heart fluttered and I thought. "This is just so wonderful. I really am falling for this guy."

Was he falling in love with me too? It certainly felt that way. If he was only after my body, why didn't he try to seduce me right there and then?

As I've said, I feel strongly that Bill sensed that our relationship was going to be something special. Also, he was obviously smart enough to know that, if you liked a woman and she was attracted to you, the coolest thing you could do was to not make your move on the first date. You then had it made on the second date.

If that was Bill's strategy, it worked like a charm. By the time he phoned me the following evening, I was completely hooked. I couldn't wait to see him again. This time, however, I had no intention of holding back—and neither did he.

Chapter 4

♦

The Passion Begins

"The heart is a mystery—not a puzzle that can be solved."
—Thomas Moore

The morning after our first date, I pretty much floated my way to work. After all the teasing and sexual stimulation, I felt both ecstatic and exhausted. My experience with Bill had been unique.

I felt that we had something between us that went beyond a sexual attraction. This was a man I wanted in my life, and I knew that he wanted me in his life. Under the circumstances, neither of us knew what that was ultimately going to mean.

These feelings were very new for me. In the past, I had gone to bed with some men simply because they turned me on physically. However, I had no interest in their intellect or ambitions. Then there were other men who turned me on because they were bright or had a great sense of humor. In those instances, I rarely felt much of a physical attraction.

A psychologist friend once told me that I was unconsciously compartmentalizing the men in my life to protect myself from getting too serious. If I ever did meet a man who had all the qualities I wanted, she cautioned, I'd find some excuse to kill the relationship.

I was beginning to think my friend was right—until Bill came along. We still hadn't made love, but I felt he had everything I was looking for in a man. Tonight would be the night when my questions would be answered. I was breathless with anticipation, wondering how it was all going to play out.

A couple of hours later, I found myself covering more of those hearings at the Department of Justice building. I was sitting in the press section, daydreaming, when I spotted Bill down on the hearing floor. He beamed a smile at me that seemed to say, "I'll be seeing you real soon."

Shortly after I got home that night, the phone rang. I had no doubt who was at the other end.

"Hey, Gennifer," Bill began. "When can we get together? I can't wait to see you again."

We decided that he would come over to my place at 8:30 the next night. I immediately began fantasizing about what was going to happen.

There was no doubt in my mind that Bill and I would make love. I was more than ready. My heart was pounding, and my eyes glazed over just thinking about it. They say that there's no stronger drug than that first flush of love, and that's exactly what I was feeling.

I can't remember very much about the following day. I do know that I went to work, but I was completely lost in thought, planning for the big night.

Which perfume would I wear? What music would I have playing?

Would we sit and talk for a while like the last time? Or would he close the door behind him and take me right into his arms? What would Bill look like with his clothes off? Would making love to him feel the way I imagined? Would he be as wonderful at seducing my body as he was at seducing my mind?

I sensed that Bill was probably going to be a magnificent lover, but you can never tell. Suddenly, I felt vulnerable. What if I really love having sex with him, and he feels disappointed?

"Hold on, Gennifer," I told myself. "This isn't the liberated girl you've worked so hard to be."

These thoughts followed me home from work. It was only 6:30 when I walked into my apartment. Plenty of time to get ready for the big night. I couldn't decide what record to play, so I just turned on the radio to a light-rock station. Then I took a shower, and sensuously rubbed my body with some Nina Ricci—my favorite perfume at the time.

What to wear? I selected a short black skirt and a matching halter top—one that did justice to my cleavage. Then I looked at myself in the mirror.

"You look great, Gennifer," I said aloud. But so what?

Looks had never been a problem for me, and men were forever trying to get me into the sack. Not only that, I had talent and a brain to boot. I thanked God for giving me so much. Still, what was it that had kept me from finding true love?

Thinking about it now, I understand that I had coated my heart with a shield of armor because I was afraid of being hurt.

Until I met Bill, I pretty much called the shots in my relationships with men—and I was very afraid of surrendering that control. To this day, I've never been rejected. Probably because the minute I sense that something's not right in a relationship, I'm out of there.

The bottom line is, I have never hung around long enough for anyone to reject me. I guess the reason for that goes back to the hurt I felt when my parents divorced after twenty years of marriage.

Before Bill, my radar for trouble was sensitive to a fault. If the smallest thing didn't feel right to me. If we were starting to argue. If he started acting a tad jealous. That was it!

Looking back, I can see that I was a prime candidate for getting involved with someone who ultimately wasn't going to be available to me. Even as I waited for Bill to arrive, I was turned on by the excitement, the danger and the pure animal magnetism I felt toward this guy.

I glanced at my watch. It was 8:30 on the nose. The doorbell was ringing. It was him.

"Take it easy, Gennifer," I reminded myself. "No need to rush anything. Just invite him into the parlor, offer him a glass of wine, and have a nice, cozy conversation. You know this is eventually going to wind up with the two of you making passionate love on your bed. So relax, and let things take their natural course."

The minute Bill hit the door, he took me in his arms, and we began to kiss passionately. Oh, well—so much for taking it slow! Bill couldn't wait a moment longer, and I wasn't inclined to object.

His full lips captured mine, and I was lost to the power and desperate hunger of his kiss. I was overtaken by a searing need that filled every part of my body and soul.

Nobody ever kissed me quite like that, not before or since. Bill wasn't an overbearing kisser, nor was he wet and sloppy. He used his tongue with an almost unbearable tenderness, yet he was confident and aggressive at the same time.

All my fantasies about Bill's deliciously sensual lips were realized at that moment. I was crazy with excitement, knowing that this was just the beginning. Suddenly, Bill lifted me up as if I were a bride on her honeymoon, and carried me into the bedroom.

Bill placed me gently on the bed, and lay there next to me, without uttering a word. I opened my arms to him. He came into them swiftly and held me close for a hot minute. Then he undid my halter. Suddenly, we were both naked, our clothes in an unruly pile on the floor.

We looked at one another longingly. Then his mouth found mine once again. He began caressing every part of me with his lips and tongue. Somehow he knew that this was exactly what I wanted from him.

His tongue moved over me with such authority that I soon slipped uncontrollably into an ecstasy I had never felt before. As intense as my passion was, I sensed that his was far stronger. Could this really be happening?

His flush skin was glittering with sweat, which conveyed his raw animal desire for me. Our kisses became desperate, as our hands grasped one another's. All that existed in that moment was our overwhelming love and need for each other.

Bill's touch was almost painfully gentle, yet I could sense that his need for me was almost violent—as if an earthquake was about to explode inside of him. I felt as if he wanted to unravel me inch by inch. To watch me lose control. To hear me beg for more.

I had always enjoyed sex, even if the act itself had rarely measured up to the anticipation. Let's face it, there is nothing magnificent about two people panting like dogs and groping each other frantically. For me, sex had usually been a nice diversion; at times it was even somewhat satisfying. But making love with Bill Clinton was a whole different ballgame.

My new lover wasn't particularly well endowed physically. Whatever he may have lacked in size, he more than made up for in passion and technique. I licked Bill's navel with my tongue just once, as if to promise what was yet to come.

Suddenly, he was on top of me, and I guided him inside. I held on tight to his pulsating shoulders as we began our primal dance. I was wild for him. Wild to feel his strong arms stroke me, to taste the heat of his reckless lust, to hear the sound of our bodies as they joined together.

We moved in slow synchronicity, as his hot kisses continued to fill my mouth with fiery delight. I felt as if I was burning up, and I would have gladly made a deal with the devil in exchange for a promise that this feeling would never end.

Was this really the same Gennifer Flowers I had known for twenty-seven years? That cool customer who prided herself on always maintaining control? That was all in the past now. Bill Clinton had rendered me a mindless, whimpering child.

After we made love that first time, both of us lay there quietly in the dark. There was no awkwardness in our silence, only the unspoken understanding of two people who had just experienced one another's core.

I've never been one to confuse a good roll in the hay with true love. Still, if what Bill and I had wasn't love, I don't know what else to call it. Whatever its name, I felt I'd found a part of me that had always been missing. There was no doubt in my mind that Bill felt the same.

Just then, Bill put his head in my lap, and I knew he what he wanted to do. I'd never been with a man who was so considerate, so eager to give me pleasure. I felt a compelling need to return the favor.

"Why don't you just lie still, and let me do all the work?" I whispered.

Bill knew I planned to use my mouth on him the way he'd used his on me. But rather than go for the ultimate moment right away, I started licking him all over his body. It gave me no end of pleasure to watch him quiver and moan as I brought him to another orgasm.

We continued to make love for several more hours, as Bill demonstrated more sexual libido than I have ever seen in a man. I'm not sure exactly how many times he came, but he seemed to be inexhaustible. I remember thinking that maybe this is the kind of drive a man needs to become president of the United States.

Much of our lovemakinging that first night was in the missionary position, which happens to be a particular favorite of mine. As time went by, things would get more kinky. But believe me, neither of us had any complaints about the more traditional stuff we were into that first night. It was a phenomenal experience by any standard.

By the time we finished making love, it was two in the morning, and I sensed that Bill would soon be leaving. We didn't talk as much as we did on that first date, but we did talk about how we loved being together, and how we would have to find ways of seeing each other regularly.

I remember sitting on my bed with Bill, as he gently stroked my hair and talked about how wonderful the night had been. Suddenly, a little chill ran through me.

Then Bill kind of shook his head and said, "I'm real sorry, but you know I can't spend the night, much as I want to. I'm going to have to be on my way in a little while."

I desperately wanted Bill to stay all night. But I knew that wasn't to be—not on this night or on any of the passionate nights we would spend together in the days, months and years to come. Bill Clinton was a married man, and I had to accept that I was the other woman.

Fifteen minutes later, Bill put on his clothes and tried to look as if he'd just come from a late political meeting. We both had a good laugh over that one. Still, I couldn't help but wonder: Hillary was known to be a very bright woman. Would she buy such a transparent charade? I certainly wouldn't if I were in her position. But, hey—I had enough of my own problems without having to worry about the lies my lover was telling his wife.

Bill and I stood at the door and looked longingly at one another. The wonders and glories of that night went beyond any words either of us could say. He took me in his arms and kissed me tenderly.

"I'll be seeing you, darling," he said.

"I intend to hold you to your word," I answered.

I had never known happiness—or misery—like this before. It was rare for me to want a lover to spend the night. Once I finished having sex with a man, I usually would find an excuse to make him leave.

Now I was feeling more unfamiliar sensations than I could handle. One night of lovemaking and I felt as though I'd formed an irretrievable bond with this man—this married man! Oh, God. What had I done to myself?

Despite my worries and reservations, I had never known happiness like this before, and I wasn't about to deny myself. If my relationship with Bill Clinton had a future, there were sure to be a lot of bumps in the road. Right then, I would have taken any risk to keep what we had found in each other's arms that night.

I'd heard rumors that Bill and Hillary were having marital problems. But I also knew that she played an important part in his political ambitions. Would he ever be willing to leave her for me? Is that even what I wanted to happen?

These were the thoughts I pondered in the waning hours of my first night of lovemaking with Bill Clinton. I was exhausted from all the sex, but there was no way I was going to fall asleep. A bolt of lightning had struck my once-predictable life, and things would never be the same again.

Chapter 5

♦

Momma's Boy
and Lover Man

"I am my beloved's, and his desire is toward me."
—from *Song of Solomon*

When two people hook up physically and emotionally the way Bill and I did, they get to know each other in a most profound way. If Bill ever owned up to our relationship, he could tell the world a whole lot about the real Gennifer Flowers. By the same token, I learned a great deal about this man who would one day become the most powerful person in the world.

One thing I found out that first night was that Bill was someone who both loved and understood women. In that sense, he was very much like his idol, John F. Kennedy. I've thought about the similarities between these two good-looking young presidents, and its effect on mine and Bill's relationship.

Both Bill and JFK grew up with fathers who were notorious womanizers. But, unlike Bill, JFK grew up with a mother who never held or kissed him—or any of her other kids for that matter.

The late Rose Kennedy stayed married to her philandering husband, but her unhappiness took a toll on the son who would become our country's most charismatic president.

Kennedy biographer Nigel Hamilton notes: "Jack was avoiding

the same domestic nightmare that [his mother] Rose was scuttling. Rose's reaction to her husband's infidelity had been to throw herself into her social activities and treat her [children] as a management exercise—a strategy Jack was too perceptive not to recognize—even as a small boy."

JFK was never known to publicly criticize his mother. However, "he would never wholly overcome his sense of abandonment and maternal deprivation, which would condemn him to a lifetime's fruitless romantic and sexual searching."

I believe that, like his boyhood idol, Bill Clinton was also fated to search endlessly for satisfying sex and true love. And, as with JFK, I'm quite sure that the key to Bill's fruitless quest lies in feelings he harbors toward his parents.

Roger Clinton, Sr., the man who reared Bill, was both an adulterer and an abusive husband. And William Blythe—Bill's biological father, who died in an auto accident before Bill was born—was a traveling salesmen whose womanizing was legendary in the territories he worked.

Virginia Kelley, Bill Clinton's late mother, had heard rumors that her first husband had been married several times before they had tied the knot. In fact, William Blythe was married to another woman when he and Virginia became husband and wife on September 3, 1943. Virginia never bothered confirming those nagging rumors about her husband's bigamy. But the press took care of that little detail soon after Bill became president.

"It appears that [William Blythe] had indeed been married before he met me," Bill Clinton's mom wrote in her autobiography. "He never told me that, nor did he tell anyone [else] in the family. So as the news accounts of his alleged three previous marriages came out, I admit I was hurt and confused; I just couldn't understand why I hadn't been told."

Whether to justify her oversight or help her son avoid further embarrassment about his personal life, Bill's mother tried to play down the revelations:

"It's hard enough to reconstruct what happened in my own life last year, much less what happened in other people's lives sixty years ago," she wrote.

"As for why [William Blythe] never told me about his previous marriages, when did he have time? Even though we were married for two years and eight months, we were actually physically together for only seven months. The rest of it, he was either off in the Army or in Chicago waiting for our house to become available. And think about it: Was he going to break the spell of [our] whirlwind romance? Was he going to drop that bombshell just as he was leaving for war? Was he going to lay it all out in writing from overseas? Was he going to spoil our reunion with such news? Was he going to risk shocking his young, pregnant wife?

"There was never a good time—and then he died."

As a veteran of numerous failed marriages herself, Virginia probably also had some empathy with her long-dead first husband to go along with any lingering anger she might have felt. But from what Bill told me, there was one part of his mother's affections that never faltered. That was the love she felt for her firstborn son.

It wasn't only that Bill was an extraordinarily handsome and good-natured child. In a house dominated by an alcoholic stepfather who was prone to physical violence, young Bill became his mother's protector.

Bill had lived through dozens of fights between his parents. As a young boy, he'd even seen his stepfather threaten his mother with a gun and shoot a hole in the wall. By the time he was fourteen, Bill was six feet tall and weighed two hundred pounds. It was then that he decided to take matters into his own hands.

One night when the family was living in the resort town of Hot Springs, Bill's mother and stepfather were in the bedroom, having another of their violent fights. This time, Bill broke down the door and confronted the much older man.

"Daddy," Bill recalled saying to his inebriated stepfather, "I've got something to say to you and I want you to stand up. If you can't stand up, I'll help you. I don't want you to lay a hand on my mother in anger ever, ever again, or you'll have to deal with me."

I can't say that Bill's mother consciously turned him into some kind of surrogate husband, but he often talked about how physical she was in expressing her affections toward him.

Bill often laughed about how his mom would grab him by the face and kiss him all over. If you wanted to get Freudian about it, you might conclude that Bill never could stay faithful to any one woman because his mother was the real love of his life.

We'll leave it to the shrinks to analyze whether or not the president has an Oedipus complex. But it's my feeling that Bill's affinity for women and his prowess as a lover came out of an extraordinarily affectionate relationship with his late mother. I also believe his taste in women was influenced by his image of her.

Bill's mother was a colorful gal who wore lots of makeup and fake eyelashes. Funny, but that's the way some members of the press have described me. Anyhow, Virginia had a whole parade of husbands and boyfriends over the years. She was also known to hit the booze pretty hard, and liked to get up on the stage at clubs and sing a drunken chorus or two with the band.

At the same time, I've got to give Bill's mom a lot of credit. She went on to become a nurse-anesthetist, which took a lot of gumption and drive on her part.

I've always thought Bill saw in me a combination of desirable qualities very much like those his mother possessed. These included intelligence, ambition, and an earthy sensuality. I've already mentioned that Bill reminded me of my father in many ways. So, I guess you could say that the ingredients for love—and disaster!—were in place from the moment we met.

Bill often talked to me about his mother, just as I talked about my folks. He would recall how good his mother was with country-style expressions, like a lot of people from Arkansas. She would say things to her young son like: "I declare, Billy. That little girl was so ugly, they had to put a pork chop around her neck to get someone to play with her."

We had a lot of good laughs over recollections like that. But the main thing that came through was: This was a man whose mother taught him to love and appreciate women in a lot of different ways.

Bill admired Hillary for her brains and ambition—just as he liked the fact that I had worked hard to forge a career as a professional singer and TV reporter. At the same time, Bill liked women who knew how to dress and act slutty when the occasion called for it. He would often tell me that I was the only woman he ever met who offered him the complete package.

At this point, we'd only had two dates, and already we knew that we were incredibly compatible—physically, mentally and emotionally. During our long affair, Bill would get to see many sides of me, just as I would get to see all the sides of this momma's boy who grew up to be a natural-born lover man. But during the days following our first night of lovemaking, I kept obsessing about what would happen next.

Now that we were lovers, would we still have the same easy rapport we discovered on our first date?

Would the second passionate night be as exciting as the first?

Our next date was only three nights later, but it felt like an eternity. Once again, Bill said he would be over at 8:30. This time, however, he was late—which I soon found out was his style.

I am generally secure about where I stand with a man, but this was different than anything I had ever known. One fantastic night, and already he had me!

Now it was 9:00, and I was getting nervous. Precious minutes were going by: 9:15 . . . 9:20. Finally, the doorbell rang. My watch read 9:33. There was Bill, dressed in a formal suit and tie.

"You're over an hour late," I complained. "I was starting to worry."

Bill flashed a wry grin, as if to remind me that he already had a mother—and a wife!

Somehow, I got his unspoken message, and we both started to laugh. Then he leaned back and began to gaze into my eyes. It was a long, piercing look that spoke volumes.

Suddenly, before I could take another breath, Bill placed an arm beneath my knees and whisked me into the bedroom as if I were weightless.

I made quick work of his tie, flinging it over my shoulder, while my mouth caressed his with a hunger I never had allowed myself to imagine. The primal feeling that overtook me the last time was even stronger on this, our second night of passion. I wanted to eat him alive so that he would forever be a part of me.

A small voice inside my head cried out: "Gennifer, keep your cool! Be rational!" But my brains were putty. Coolness and rationality were the last things I cared about.

I somehow managed to steal a breath, when our mouths embraced once more. Bill offered a weak protest as I tore open his shirt, and I was momentarily distracted by a fantasy of what he must have been thinking:

"Oh, shit—what will Hillary say when I come home with a torn shirt?"

"To hell with Hillary," I screamed, silently. "To hell with everyone and everything in the world outside this room!"

I could see that Bill no longer cared that his neatly tailored formal shirt was now torn to pieces. We had both abandoned all thoughts of anything, save devouring each other.

What was most unbelievable for me was the sense that my passion was eclipsed by his.

Could that actually be? I wondered. What living thing could feel something stronger than the volcanos that were erupting throughout my body and igniting my soul?

Now we were both grasping each other on the bed. I could feel his mouth embrace my lace-covered breasts, as his strong hands moved gingerly under my skirt, searching for my pulsing pleasure spot.

A moment of elegant calm overtook me, and I began to moan

plaintively, waiting for him to enter. Then he suddenly shifted position and began to kiss my thighs.

I had never known a man so eager to use his mouth for pleasure or so skilled at it. Only later did I fully appreciate what my lover was trying to tell me: That giving me satisfaction took precedence over getting it himself. For the moment, I was content to lean back and enjoy the delicious gift I was receiving.

As I lay there, the warmest, most wonderful memories began to flood my brain. Nothing I'd felt in the past could ever approach the intimate moments we were sharing.

Then I heard myself moaning again, this time more rhythmically than before. As my song-poem reached its crescendo, Bill pulled his mouth away ever so gently, and paused to catch his breath.

Now it was I who was putting my head in his lap, and kissing his thigh, suggestively. Bill understood what I had in mind—and he was genuinely appreciative. Neither of us gave a hoot about gaining control or playing tit for tat. Each of us wanted desperately to satisfy the other.

During that first glorious night, I had learned the secret spots where my lover most enjoyed being kissed. Now I hoped to use that knowledge to give him more pleasure that he'd ever known.

Bill rubbed my head gently, as I worked my womanly magic on him. His satisfaction drizzled down as I completed my joyous task. The sound of his ecstasy subsided, and another exquisite moment of silence passed between us. We both knew what was coming next.

Once again, his lips seized mine, and I was lost to the power and desperate hunger of his kiss. My knees gave way, as a searing need overtook my being. I guided him inside me, and we were again entwined in the ancient dance we had somehow invented.

Bill clung to me with powerful hands that were, at the same time, gentle as a butterfly's kiss. Neither of us could bear the thought that these two ecstatic dancers might not have much of a future. Still, I asked for no promises of an enduring relationship or a secure tomorrow.

Bill and I both knew that he could not offer such assurances to me—much as he may have wanted to. As I lay in his arms, his body gave silent testament of his need for me, and later he would declare his love in so many words.

As we settled into seeing each other on a regular basis, Bill learned to play me like a finely tuned Stradivarius, and I became skilled at doing the same for him. We stroked one another's body and mind.

In time, I felt that we had connected on every level. The two of us could always talk and laugh together, regardless of whether we were making love.

Even during those first hot months as lovers, there were times Bill would come over, and all we would do was talk and listen to music. If I would give even the slightest hint that I wasn't in the mood to get into something physical, Bill would never push the issue.

Bill craved intense sexual contact. At the same time, he always seemed far more interested in mutuality and two-way communication than in controlling or pushing me into any specific sexual act. Bill Clinton may have a voracious sexual appetite, yet I could never see him forcing himself on a woman, as some people have alleged.

One reason Bill has gotten so far politically is that he has an almost insatiable drive to please. That's the way he is with women too. He'll say and do anything to bring you around to his way of thinking, but I can't envision Bill ever trying to push himself on someone who didn't want him.

Especially during those early days of our affair, Bill was genuinely concerned with my happiness. He was always extremely considerate and tender in all his dealings with me. Bill knew that I had never experienced such intense pleasure with any other lover—and swore that the same was true for him.

Our bodies and souls had come together in a very profound way. We both knew that our relationship was fragile, which made the time we had together even more precious. Both of us desperately wanted to make our love last. Unfortunately, neither of us had a clue as to how we were going to accomplish that neat little trick.

Chapter 6

♦

A Dream That Could Never Come True

"I am opposed to abortion and to government funding of abortions. We should not use state funds on abortions because so many people think abortion is wrong."

—Bill Clinton

So there I was, head-over-heels in love with the married attorney general of Arkansas. And there he was, head-over-heels in love with me.

"Where do we go from here?" I often found myself thinking out loud. "Should I start planning for a future together, or just take things one night a time?"

It didn't take long to answer that question in my mind. Only a fool would start planning long term under these circumstances. Still, when a woman finds the right man, it's only natural to want him with her all the time. Or is it?

There were so many potential complications for Bill and me. He had only been married to Hillary for less than two years, and they were as yet childless. Divorce was still a possibility for Bill—at least that's what I thought. If that happened, the coast would be clear for us to get married. But was that what I really wanted?

I had been busting my tail for years, trying to get a show business career off the ground. Even if Bill was willing to dump Hillary for me, I wasn't at all sure I was ready to assume the responsibilities

of being the wife of an attorney general who aspired to be governor—and eventually president.

Not only that, people in Little Rock were already whispering
about our affair. Could Bill's political aspirations survive the scandal of throwing over his wife for his mistress?

Bill had talked Hillary into relocating to Arkansas, a move she
was not very enthusiastic about making. But Bill Clinton had a
foothold in his home state, and knew that getting into local politics
was the best and fastest way to realize his—and her—greater ambitions. Not only that, Bill needed someone like Hillary to further his
heady objectives.

"Theirs was a fortuitous, even extraordinary pairing," one writer
has noted. "[Bill Clinton] is the first to concede that without
[Hillary's] determination, stability, and focus, he might have never
realized his dream. . . .

"He wanted political success. She wanted political power. Intelligent, talented, and committed—some would say driven—to change
the face of American society, she was willing to redirect her own
ambitions and efforts so that both might have what they sought.
On her own, she could go far, but . . . the odds favored *him* [sic]
going farther."

I firmly believe that Bill and Hillary had forged this contract
long before we met. Apparently Hillary was willing to put up with
her husband's cheating. But she never would have tolerated his leaving her without trying to exact some revenge. And, frankly, I wouldn't
have blamed her.

Had she been so inclined, Hillary could have delivered a fatal
blow to Bill's political ambitions—and he knew it. Nevertheless, I
wasn't ready to give up hope.

There were other things Bill could do besides politics. He was a
talented lawyer. What if he went into teaching or private practice?
He would still have a rewarding career, and the two of us could be
together.

Looking back, it's obvious that my brain knew what my heart

could not admit. As much as Bill loved me, nothing and nobody was ever going to stand in the way of his quest for political power. Somehow, I would have to face the reality that *this* was a mistress more tempting than I could ever be, but it wasn't easy.

There's a fine line separating optimism from self-delusion, and I've crossed that line several times where Bill Clinton is concerned. I can't say that Bill led me on with false promises, yet he somehow managed to keep that flame of hope burning in my heart.

The two of us would be lying in bed, and he'd say: "Wouldn't it be great if we could spend time in the country and take long walks together? One of these days, I know we are going to do that."

I had certainly been around long enough to know that a lot of men will lie in order to heighten a romantic moment. Even so, I loved to hear Bill share those thoughts with me, and he always sounded so sincere.

I still don't know for sure if Bill's words were heartfelt, or if he was just trying to keep me hanging on emotionally. Either way, I couldn't let go of the belief that he was planning for a time that we could be together as a couple, unencumbered by the complication of his marriage.

For the most part, I tried not to dwell on what was going to happen down the road. Instead, I placed my focus on the close bond we had forged and the passionate lovemaking that just kept getting better and better.

I never made a conscious decision to stop seeing other men, but I soon discovered that I had no interest in being with anyone but Bill. Outside of work, he was my life. Then, something happened that would shatter all my dreams.

In the early part of December, 1977, I was hosting a TV interview show on KARK. One of my guests was a woman who headed an abortion clinic in Little Rock. The topic of abortion was no less controversial back then than it is now. I dug right in to the pros and cons of that delicate issue.

As I sat under the hot lights of that TV set, glibly working both sides of the abortion question, I had no idea how close to home that topic actually was. For, at that very moment, I was pregnant with William J. Clinton's baby.

Two weeks after that interview, my period was late. This was unusual for me. My cycles had always been as regular as clockwork, so I immediately called my doctor and made an appointment.

"What's up, Doc?" I asked, as he examined me. "Please don't tell me I'm pregnant."

"We'll have to wait a few days for the test results," he answered. "Have you been using birth control during intercourse?"

Unfortunately, the answer to that question was no.

When Bill and I first started sleeping together, I was using a diaphragm, but found it to be a real drag. The device was so clumsy. More often than not, it would pop out when I tried to use it. Bill hated using a condom, and I also preferred making love without one. Still, I was concerned about getting pregnant.

"Not to worry," Bill insisted over and over again. "Hillary and I have tried to have a baby, and nothing has happened. I'm pretty sure I'm sterile."

This was hardly scientific proof, but it was what I wanted to hear. So, Bill and I continued to make love three or four nights a week without any protection.

Naturally, I didn't go into all these details for my doctor, nor did I reveal the identity of my lover. All I said was, "Yes, I'm afraid that I did have unprotected sex quite a few times over the past few months."

I had been seeing that same doctor for years, and knew that he wasn't one to moralize about my sex life. Still, he clearly wasn't very happy with me.

"Okay, Gennifer," the doctor said glumly. "I'll be in touch as soon as the test results come back."

Two days later I got the call: I was pregnant!

Whatever confusion I felt before was small potatoes now. This was a genuine crisis—one that was bound to have serious consequences, whatever the ultimate outcome.

I was filled with mixed emotions. Like any woman, I felt the joy of having life grow inside my body. But, by then, I was pushing thirty, and had built a life around being an independent career woman. No way was I going to have a child without a husband and father to help care for her or him. Still, this child belonged to the man I loved.

I tried to go through all the possible scenarios in my mind. Did I really want a child—even under the best of circumstances? Would my pregnancy be the catalyst for Bill to leave Hillary? I didn't really think so, much as my heart wanted to believe otherwise.

At that point in time, Bill wanted to run for governor of Arkansas—and he needed Hillary's help. The 1978 gubernatorial election was just around the corner, and Bill was going to have to make his intentions known. There had been no public announcement yet, though Bill had already told me that he was definitely going to run. How would this play into his—and my—decision about what to do with this baby?

These were just some of the thoughts running through my mind, as I wrestled with what was going to be one of the toughest decisions of my life.

A couple of nights later, Bill came over to see me. We sat in those same two antique maplewood chairs in my parlor, just as we had on our first date. It seemed like years had passed, though it had only been a few months.

"Bill," I began, "there's something I need to tell you." Then I took a deep breath for courage. "I'm pregnant with our baby."

When he heard the news, Bill didn't act shocked. He took my hand and asked, "Are you okay?"

I burst into tears, relieved that his first response was concern for my welfare. In my worst fantasies, I pictured Bill reacting with anger and accusing me of lying about his being the father.

"Well, I'm sick as a dog," I answered, gathering some of my

composure. "The smell of almost everything makes me want to throw up, and my whole body feels puffy and sore. But don't you worry. I'll be fine."

After that, we sat there and made small talk for a while. If Bill had any serious intentions toward me, that was the time to make them known. I purposely stretched the conversation out to give him time to say the words I so desperately wanted to hear, but those words never came.

Bill's concern for me was that of a caring friend, and it did help me feel somewhat better. He held my hand and promised that he would help in any way he could. But he never said: "Gennifer, I'll get a divorce. Then we'll get married and live as one happy family."

It broke my heart not to hear those words, but at least I knew what my course of action would have to be. I told Bill then that I wanted to have an abortion as soon as possible. Bill tried to act impassive, but I'm sure he was relieved.

I still hoped that he would at least express some regret that we couldn't have a child together, or say how nice it might have been if circumstances were different. But, no, he wasn't going to grant me even that much. It was now crystal clear that marrying me was the farthest thing from his mind.

Bill gave me the two hundred dollars I needed for the abortion, and I called the woman I had interviewed on TV. She helped me maintain a degree of privacy when I went to her clinic, but it was still a traumatic experience.

When the dreaded day came, I drove myself to the clinic. I could have used some company, but I didn't want to tell anyone about my condition. Other than Bill, my doctor and the woman from the clinic, nobody knew about the pregnancy I was about to terminate.

If anyone found out that I was aborting Bill Clinton's baby, it would have surely killed his chances to become governor. I felt deceived and deserted by Bill, yet my instinct was to protect him from scandal. After all, what could be nearly as important as Bill Clinton's quest for power? Certainly not Gennifer Flowers or the unborn child whose precious life was about to be extinguished.

It was 2 P.M. on a cold, Wednesday afternoon. I pulled into the clinic parking lot, and walked into the reception area. The room had a sterile, institutional look, and the medicinal smells turned my stomach. There were several other women sitting around, trying to read magazines as they waited to be called.

I tried to remain inconspicuous, as I looked over some of the women and wondered about their stories. I noticed a pretty, young Latina woman seated next to a frumpy, redneck-looking housewife.

I cut my survey short. What did it matter how these women looked, or how they ended up here? The result was the same. Each of us was about to take the same painful step.

After a few minutes, several of us were called in for a group counseling session. I tried to act as if I were listening attentively, but I don't recall hearing a single word she said.

A half hour later, I was flat on my back, legs up in those hateful surgical stirrups. The middle-aged male doctor standing over me scrupulously avoided making eye contact. He just stood there, with his impersonal tool, ready to enter my body and extinguish the most personal thing on God's earth—the life of an unborn baby.

The abortion procedure was demeaning and extremely painful. After it was over, I went into an adjoining room, sat in a chair, and sobbed bitterly. I don't know what was worse, the physical pain or the heartbreak.

"Oh, Bill," my heart cried out. "Wasn't there another way we could have handled this situation? Couldn't I have borne the child and given him up for adoption?"

Such speculation was fruitless now. The deed was done. It was all over! I drove home, and took to my bed. It was a little after six when the phone rang.

"Gennifer, it's Bill. How did it go? Are you okay?"

I let a moment of heavy silence pass before answering.

"Now that you ask, I feel awful. Killing that baby was the worst experience of my life."

"I'm really very sorry it worked out this way," he said, sincerely. "I'll call again tomorrow. If there's anything I can do—anything at all. . . ."

There are some scars that can never heal completely. But on the surface, I had made a quick recovery. And, despite all that had happened, I was not inclined to end our relationship. I guess you can say I was blinded by love—temporarily insane! While I didn't hold out much hope that Bill and I would ever have a life together, I had no desire to see anyone else.

There was, however, one important change brought about by the trauma of my abortion. Never again would I have sex without using birth control. Since diaphragms only work if you insert them, I switched to birth control pills—and took them faithfully. No way was I ever going to go through the horror of an abortion again.

For the next few months, Bill and I went on pretty much like before. Then one night he walked in beaming. He had some big news to share.

"Hillary is pregnant. I'm going to be a daddy. Gennifer, isn't that great?"

I tried to smile, but I was deeply insulted. There he was, on cloud nine because he was going to be a father. And I'm thinking, "You bastard. I was pregnant with your baby, and that meant absolutely nothing to you."

A part of me was genuinely happy for Bill. After all, I cared about him as a person. But at the time, I was deeply in love with him, and this was a real slap in the face.

It was as if he was saying: "Hey, honey, I'm chalking up still another victory in my life. You're a real nice person, but let's put your own concerns on the back burner."

It took me a while to absorb all this. On some level, I felt that Bill had abandoned me when I had my abortion. But that night, the abandonment felt complete. I knew with all certainty that Bill and I would never be any more than cheating husband and mistress.

The next morning, I went out for a walk. While passing a nearby church, I gazed at the sidewalk, and spotted what I imagined to be some grains of rice left over from a wedding—someone else's wedding, not mine.

I couldn't help but compare those grains of rice and the state in which I now found myself. I felt as if my whole existence could have easily been blown away by a stiff wind.

"Face it, girl," I told myself, "This was a dream that never could come true. But don't let self-pity overtake you. Get a grip on your emotions and move on."

A short time later, I left Little Rock—and Bill Clinton—to pursue my interests as a singer. I knew that I had to quit being so entrenched in his world and get on with my own life.

That's exactly what I did.

I was a cheerleader for Brinkley High School in Brinkley, Arkansas for several years. I am the one in front, doing the split.

This was in Brinkley, Arkansas in the 60's when I was President of the Young Arkansans for Rockerfeller. This was our YAR group. I am the one in the center.

Gennifer Flowers
and
Easy Living

P.O. BOX 1232   501 375—4032

LITTLE ROCK, ARKANSAS 72203

This was one of my bands in Arkansas. We played at the Sheraton Hotel, among other places.

I was 25 years old.

This is a promotional shot taken in 1973. It was only a few short years until I would meet Bill. This is how I looked—with black hair—when he met me.

This is an entertainment promotional photo taken while I was singing at the Fairmont Hotel in Dallas, Texas in 1980.

This is the front of the Justice Building with the Capitol Building in the background in Little Rock. It was in the Justice Building that Bill first asked me for my telephone number. I was there covering a story as a news reporter for KARK-TV, an NBC affiliate in Little Rock, Arkansas.

This is the Governor's Mansion in Little Rock. I sang in the backyard for a pre-game football party. Bill tried to have sex with me in the bathroom.

This is one of a pair of antique chairs in my Little Rock apartment where Bill and I enjoyed many pleasurable hours sitting and talking.

Entrance to Quapaw Tower. Bill came in through the front door until a security guard told people in the building he was visiting Gennifer Flowers.

This is my balcony with the awning at Quapaw Tower Apartments. This is where I would watch for Bill to jog or drive by so that I could go prop the side door open for his entry when he would visit.

This is the side door at Quapaw Tower in Little Rock that I would prop open with a newspaper so that Bill could enter unobserved.

Bill and I shared many glorious sexual experiences in my bed.

I still have this sexy black nightie that Bill gave me.

My white nightie-and-garter ensemble was a particular favorite of Bill's during our sexcapades.

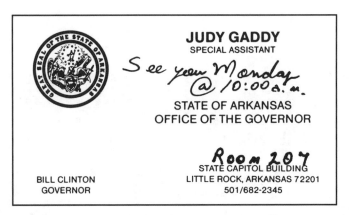

JUDY GADDY
SPECIAL ASSISTANT

See you Monday @ 10:00 a.m.

STATE OF ARKANSAS
OFFICE OF THE GOVERNOR

Room 207
STATE CAPITOL BUILDING
LITTLE ROCK, ARKANSAS 72201
501/682-2345

BILL CLINTON
GOVERNOR

Judy Gaddy gave me this card as a reminder of our appointment. She was assisting Bill Clinton in getting me the state job.

Bill and I made a concerted effort to update each other on the current media crisis. Bill called me often while on the campaign trail. This is a number he left on my answering machine.

LABORATORY REPORT

AMERICAN
BIOMEDICAL
CORPORATION

5040

The Clinical Laborator
1221 Westpark Dr.
Little Rock, Ark.

Dr. K.M.Kreth
417 N. Univ.
Little Rock, Ark.

RECEIVED	REPORTED
12-20-77	—
COLLECTED	TIME

DOCTOR	PATIENT NAME	AGE	SEX	PATIENT IDENTIFICATION
	Jeninifer Flowers			7684

REQ. NO	TEST REQUESTED	SPECIMEN CONDITION
	PG Test	Urine

GLUCOSE 65-115 mg/dl	BUN 5-25 mg/dl	CREATININE 0.7-1.4 mg/dl	BUN/CREAT. RATIO 7-18	CHOLESTEROL 150-300 mg/dl	TRIGLYCERIDE 30-150 mg/dl	IRON 50-180 µg/dl	SODIUM 135-145 meq/l	POTASSIUM 3.5-5.2 meq/l	CHLORIDE 97-108 meq/l	CO₂ 22-32 meq/l	ELECTROLYTE BALANCE

URIC ACID 2.3-8.1 mg/dl	TOTAL PROTEIN 6.0-8.0 g/dl	ALBUMIN 3.5-5.5 g/dl	GLOBULIN 0.5-4.5 g/dl	A/G RATIO 1.2-2.2	TOTAL BILIRUBIN 0.1-1.2 mg/dl	ALK. PHOS. 30-100 U/l	LDH 100-225 U/l	SGOT 0-40 U/l	SGPT 0-50 U/l	CALCIUM 8.5-10.5 mg/dl	PHOSPHORUS 2.0-4.0 mg/dl

T3 UPTAKE 22-35 %	T4 5.0-12.0 µg/dl	T7 1.1-4.2	T3 BY RIA 85-220 ng/dl	TSH 1-10 µU/ml	GGTP 0-45 U/l	CEA ng/ml	B₁₂ 300-1000 pg/ml	DIGOXIN 0.5-2.5 ng/ml	RENIN ng/ml/hr	FOLIC ACID 2.3-15.6 ng/ml	AUSTRALIA ANTIGEN neg.

WBC X10³ M 4.8-10.8 F 4.8-10.8	RBC X10⁶ M 4.7-6.1 F 4.2-5.4	HGB g/dl M 14-18 F 12-16	HCT % M 42-52 F 37-47	MCV µ³ M 80-94 F 81-99	MCH µµg M 27-31 F 27-31	MCHC % M 32-36 F 32-36	ANA neg.	RUBELLA	ANTIBODY SCREEN	VDRL non-reactive	ASO 0-160 Todd Units

SEG	BAND	LYMPH	MONO	EOSIN	BASO	PLATELETS	LITHIUM 0.4-0.8 meq/l	DILANTIN 10-20 µg/ml	PHENOBARB 15-40 µg/ml	FTA-ABS non-react	VMA 1.0-8.0 mg/24 hr.

OTHER TEST RESULTS/COMMENTS:

PG Test   *Positive*

DEC 20 12 58 PM '77

A laboratory report from my doctor in Little Rock verified that I was pregnant. I knew it was Bill Clinton's baby, but had to make a painful decision to terminate the pregnancy.

October 29, 1991

To Management,

When I came in today for lunch, someone had entered my apartment. There was
no yellow receipt slip left in my home to let me know why someone had
entered. This is the second time in approximately two weeks that this has
happened.

In the future, I insist that ANYTIME my aparment is entered by anyone that
is a part of your organization ,I be left a notice to that effect, as well
as a notice on my outside door knob.

I would appreciate your investigating this matter and putting a stop to
anyone entering my apartment without leaving appropriate paper work
explaining why it was necessary to enter my home.

Gennifer Flowers
#M105
Forest Place Apartments

This letter proves my concern that unknown persons were entering my Little Rock apartment illegally.

Dear Miss Flowers

My grandchildren and I are such admirers of yours for being so honest & forthright. Good for you! I only recently discovered celebrities often times will answer requests from fans. I used to collect autographs in my youth, but always obtained them in person (John Wayne, Amelia Earhart, JFK and Thomas Edison to name a few.)

I'm writing to request a signed photo for each of my two grandchildren if possible. I've looked in Gresham and can't find any photos of you. I realize there's cost involved, so if you charge for such things, please let me know. Their names are Pal (short for Palmer) and Honey.

I'll be 88 this month and I'm having a great deal of fun getting back into collecting for the youngsters. Thank you so much for your time.

Warm regards and best wishes.

I receive about 100 letters like these per week. I certainly appreciate all of the warm thoughts and support these people express. The names and addresses have been deleted to ensure privacy.

Dear Miss Flowers:

How hard it must be for a woman to find herself in a relationship with a married
man. You dedicated your book, "Passion & Betrayal" to all the women that find themselves
in such a position. Perhaps you might know that there are, married men, such as
I, to be in love with another woman, not his wife, as I find myself to be.

There is strong fellings, even today, that if a man, married or not, has an affair
that he is allowed to sow, "wild oats", but the woman is now thought to be damaged
goods, a hoar, but as you say, and so do I, "It takes two to Tango."

The use of the word, "Bimbo" abhors me and is offensive to imply women as being
such.

You had to find out the hard way that persons of rank, members of Congress, judges,
law enforcement personel, even to President Clinton follow the same motto, "Be sincere
whether you mean it or not", and the first rule of duty is for the betterment of
themselves.

Bill Clinton is made of carboard, he is a known liar, a man of little to no principles,
what few brains he has are programmed by Hilary, and all the reports of Bill's feebleness
as governor of Arkansas, were known, before the election, not believed by the American
public, even your story in "Penthouse" was not able to stop him from being President
because the country could not take another four years of George Bush.

You are to be commended to tell you story in your book, "Passion & Betrayal". I
hope you have truly found the right man in your life - Finis.

Hopefully I have been able to convey to you that I admire your honesty to be able
to tell your side of the story as painful as it was.

Dear Ms. Flowers,   5-26-94

     I watched you last night on "Rolanda", and I want you to
know that you are to be applauded for hanging in there while
Rolanda verbally insulted you. (Believe me, a letter goes out
to her today as well, and it is not a friendly one!)
          I am a very good judge of character, and I believe
you, Ms. Flowers. There is no question about it. How can there
be? The presidents moral character speaks for itself. You
need not say a word to prove anything to me. But, the
American public seems to be in denial... no one wants to
accept the truth. Instead, they point fingers, and turn up
their noses in disgust at the ladies, blaming it all on
them. Hang in there, baby. Truth will prevail!
          God will be with you through this. I heard
you admit you've sinned. I take it you're Christian.
Well, sister, congratulations on finding the One True Source
of peace. (This world is not going to give it to you — that's
for sure!) I am just one American voice, but I am
behind you, all the way. I know there are many more
that feel as I do, as well.   ❀   Take Care, God Bless.

My dog Buttons was a joy and—unlike some people—remained loyal when it mattered most.

Chapter 7

◆

Stolen Moments
with Mr. Kinky

"Did you know Bill Clinton competed in the Olympics? His events were backpedaling, issue straddling, and freestyle waffling."
—David Letterman

W hen I first left Little Rock, I had pretty much decided that it would be best for me to cut off all ties with Bill. Being with him could only remind me of a painful time that I would prefer to forget. Although I still loved him, it was hard to pretend that he hadn't shattered my dreams.

I had relocated to Oklahoma, then Texas, and my singing career quickly got back on track. During those years in the late 1970s and early 1980s, I worked at some top-notch venues and, for a time, was on the road as a backup singer and opening act with country music superstar Roy Clark. Through it all, Bill kept calling and pursuing me.

Despite my misgivings, I continued to stay in contact with Bill, but things had changed. We still made passionate love whenever we could find a way to be in the same geographic area, but I had pretty much cleansed myself of any and all serious expectations. At least that's what I thought.

During the course of our twelve-year affair, Bill I and were together hundreds of times. This, despite our sometimes not seeing each other for months when I was singing on the road or when I wasn't living in Arkansas.

I can recall many wonderful nights of lovemaking, but a few stand out as all-time greats. Some of our most passionate encounters came after we had been apart for a long while.

There was one time in particular I recall in 1980, while I was living and working in Fort Worth, Texas. Bill, who was now governor of Arkansas, was in town for a political conference, and he came by Remington's Restaurant, where I was singing, to pick up my apartment key. I had about an hour left before my last set was over and I could fly into his arms.

Bill and I hadn't been together for months, and it was wonderful to see him again. The anticipation of him waiting in my bed was turning me on to no end. As a singer, I have a special way of expressing my feelings through music. Even though Bill wasn't there for the set, it was as if my songs were sending messages of love straight from my heart to his. I remember singing "Reunited," "Other Lady," and "What Are You Doing for the Rest of Your Life?"

By the time I finished the last song, it was almost midnight, and I couldn't wait to get out of there. People were trying to talk to me, but in my mind Bill and I were already making love. It was only about four miles from Remington's to my place, but the ten-minute drive felt like an eternity.

When I arrived home, Bill was lying in my bed with most of his clothes on. I smiled at him suggestively, as he took me in his arms. I knew we would begin undressing one another in a minute, and I struggled to clear my mind of all hurtful thoughts.

By now, the Clintons' daughter Chelsea was a toddler and I had no illusions about Bill leaving Hillary for me. To my surprise, he would still sometimes talk dreamily about a time in the future when the two of us would be together. Though I knew this was just a fantasy, the love we felt for each other was very real.

For tonight, I wanted no part of the past—nor would I entertain thoughts of an uncertain future. Bill sighed as he folded his lips around mine, and I knew the only thing that mattered were these precious moments together.

Then, Bill began kissing me on the mouth, and I was amazed at how this simple show of affection could still set my body aflame. Would I ever get over this man? Did I really want to get over him?

In a few short hours, he would be gone. We might not see each other for months. This was anything but a healthy situation, yet it was much too late to put my heart and body into reverse. My only choice was to push all fears aside, and try to extract every drop of pleasure the moment had to offer.

"What are we doing?" I asked. But, of course, I knew the answer. We were continuing a dance we could never possibly complete—and that unspoken truth only made our passion more intense.

Suddenly Bill began devouring my lips with a hunger and need he'd been holding inside for months. Our kisses became desperate, as our hands began groping one another in search of those secret places known only to us.

In an instant, we had taken off each other's clothes, and it was as if we'd never been apart. The pure physical need we had for one another was overwhelming. I had never felt such a consuming passion—not even during those first searing nights in Little Rock.

After an hour of intense, satisfying lovemaking, I was overcome for a brief moment by a sense of loss.

"Oh, Bill," my heart wanted me to beg. "Will you really be going so soon? Then what will become of me?"

As we lay naked, side by side, we talked and laughed into the night, as we often did after an exhilarating session of lovemaking. I can't recall our exact conversation on that particular night, but Bill often expounded on a variety of topics during our twelve years together.

I usually tried to discourage conversations about Hillary, especially during such intense nights as the one in Fort Worth. Nevertheless, he often felt the need to talk about her, and most of what he had to say was derogatory.

Bill had always led me to believe that he and Hillary didn't have much of a sex life, and even confirmed a rumor I'd heard that she was having an affair with a woman.

"Hell," Bill laughed when I asked about the gossip. "She's eaten more pussy than I have." During the course of our long conversations, Bill often made telling comments about a variety of public figures. Let me share some that come to mind.

- *Vince Foster:* According to Washington gossip, White House counsel Vincent Foster, a one-time partner of Hillary Clinton's in Little Rock's Rose law firm, was alleged to have committed suicide because Hillary had broken off an affair with him. Not so, according to Bill Clinton—who told me that he was certain Vincent was far too gentle for Hillary. Bill also revealed that Hillary never liked Foster and resented his friendship with the future president.
- Vice President *Al Gore* now holds the number-two office in the land and has become Clinton's partner in the effort to "reinvent government." But they weren't always such close pals. Upset that his try for the 1988 Democratic presidential nomination hardly got off the ground, Bill Clinton disparaged Gore and other competitors who outdistanced him that year. As far as Bill was concerned, the future vice president was "Gore the Bore." "That man is the most boring son of a bitch I've ever seen," he confided.
- Missouri Congressman *Dick Gephardt* was "the house drip."
- Former California Governor *Jerry Brown*—who mounted the most serious challenge to Clinton during the 1992 Democratic primaries—had "a big mouth and an even bigger ego."

Bill's and my night of passion at my Fort Worth apartment took place during the last days of *Jimmy Carter's* presidency. At one point while we were talking, Bill turned on the TV to catch something on the news. The first image to appear on the screen was that of Jimmy and Rosalynn Carter holding hands.

Bill joked that he could hardly imagine the Carters in bed together. "I'm sure they have sex," he said, "but it must be the kind of polite 'white person's sex' some black comedians parody in their routines."

Bill then commented that if any of those comedians wanted to see white people who know how to have some hot-blooded sex, "they ought to check out you and me sometimes."

A few minutes later, Bill turned the TV off, and we continued to laugh and talk. After a while, Bill fell asleep, but I continued chattering away. I could talk to Bill forever, and there were so many things I wanted to share after all this time apart. As always, it was not to be.

Even though Hillary wasn't with Bill on this trip, he was traveling with a group of political people, and had to keep up appearances.

It was almost three A.M. when Bill left. I would have cried like a baby if I wasn't so tired. At least I knew that the next night, I'd be able to lose myself by singing some melancholy love songs, and dreaming about the next time Bill and I could share another one of our steamy, bittersweet nights of love.

As much as possible, I tried not to focus too much on my profound feelings of love for Bill. It was far easier for both of us to concentrate on sex, and that's what we did.

Bill is the most sex-crazed man I've ever known. His tastes in sex are incredibly varied to the point of being kinky. In any case, he never seemed to get enough—which was usually fine by me.

Bill loved for me to wear erotic clothes, but was cautious not to buy them for me when we were both in Little Rock. Since all of our rendezvous were now taking place out of town and away from curious eyes, he had started buying me sexy lingerie.

Bill got turned on by picking out the objects of clothing and fantasizing about how they would look on me. I still have many of Bill's erotic gifts, and would never wear them when I'm with another man.

One of my favorite gifts from Bill is a tiny black teddy with thin straps and a lace inset that reveals just enough of my breasts to be provocative. Bill loved it when I put that on, but he got even more excited when I took it off.

Bill often asked me to model the sexy lingerie he bought, and I was happy to oblige. I would dance and move around suggestively on the bed, as he lay there playing with himself. My sheer teddies revealed every voluptuous curve—which really excited him.

Bill could only stand watching me for a few short moments. Soon, he would get so aroused that he couldn't stand it any longer. Then, he would gently take my hand, pull me to the floor, and slip off the teddy. The feel of his hands caressing my skin made me tremble with excitement, as I felt the passion surging through him.

Early on, we had thought of pet names for one another. I was his "Pookie" and he was my "Baby" or "Darlin." We also had pet names for our private parts. I called my honeypot "Precious," and he called his penis "Willard."

"Why did you choose to call it Willard?" I once asked him. "Because I always liked that name," he said. "Anyway, Willard is a longer version of Willy!"

Sometimes, Bill would call me on the telephone, and I could always tell if other people were in the room with him, because the first thing he would ask was, "How are the girls?"

I would laugh, knowing he was referring to my breasts.

"They are just fine," I would answer with a chuckle. Then I would return the favor by asking him, "How are the boys?"

Speaking of the telephone, Bill also had a thing for phone sex. I wouldn't be at all surprised if he calls one of those sex phone line numbers when live bodies are in short supply. The reason I say that is because, when we were apart, Bill would often try to get me to talk dirty so that he could have an orgasm at the other end of the phone.

Unlike Bill, I have never been big on phone sex. I could never have a climax that way, though I did sometimes fake it so that he could complete his fantasy.

Bill would never come out and say, "Let's have phone sex." Instead, it usually went something like this: We'd be having a nice conversation. Suddenly, Bill would lower his voice, and I knew he was about to start getting into it.

"What are you wearing?" he would ask.

"Nothing, except for the black teddy you bought me," I'd answer. "I've got my hand on the girls and I'm about to rub them very softly."

"Do you know what I wish?" Bill would ask breathlessly.

"No, what?"

"God, I wish you were here, and could do the same to the boys."

We would go on like that for a while, until finally, Bill would come. Sometimes I would be the one to provoke matters by saying erotic things to him. But ultimately I found our phone sex to be frustrating.

When Bill and I were together, sex was almost always incredibly good. Trying to get it on over the phone wound up being a painful reminder that we were not together. Instead of satisfying me, I found myself longing for the real thing.

Even though I sometimes refused to get into the phone sex, I was usually an eager co-conspirator in many of the things Bill wanted to do when were together, though I did have my limits.

Bill was always looking for ways to enhance our sexual pleasure, and I have to give him credit: The man was never caught short when it came to inventing interesting ideas for us to try.

At one point, he suggested dripping ice on my body. The first cold drop sent a little shiver down my spine. Soon, he had me moaning with pleasure as he stood over my naked body and dripped the icy water onto my nipples.

As Bill continued to drip ice all over my naked body, I heard myself begging him to make love to me. Instead, he continued to tease and torture me, forcing me to wait until I thought I would black out. Finally, he entered me, and made love to me with a passion more fiery than any I had ever felt—even from him. Soon, our voices were echoing the song lovers sing in a moment of simultaneous orgasm.

The ice had proved a marvelous accessory, but Bill was forever looking to try something new. It seemed like the more I agreed to indulge Bill's fantasies, the kinkier he would try to get.

I once told Bill about a film I saw in which a woman had dripped hot candle wax all over her lover. Bill actually seemed to like the idea, and asked me to do the same to him. I had heard that some powerful men in politics and business enjoy having women inflict pain on them. Still, dripping hot wax over a man's body struck me as excessive.

"That sounds like it would be real painful," I told him. "And I just can't bring myself to do anything that might actually hurt you."

Bill didn't push it. But, a few nights later, he asked me to spank him during sex play. I wasn't averse to the idea of what seemed like a harmless game, and I did want to please him. So I agreed. I think Bill sensed that inflicting pain wasn't my thing, but he did get a tremendous charge out of having me slap his behind.

One of Bill's kinky games ties in with some of the jokes in the press about Bill's love of food. At one point in our sex play, we used food as a sensuous toy.

I had a little plastic honey jar that was shaped like a bear. Bill would take that plastic bear and slowly squeeze the honey all over my body. Then, he'd slowly rub it all over me. Before long we'd both be completely turned on. At which point, he'd carry me into bed and we'd make delicious love.

Bill and I also loved to sit on the floor and play sex games using different types of food. Bill would blindfold me, then go to the kitchen and look for foods that would feel sensuous in my mouth.

I found myself getting tremendously aroused when he'd slowly pour juice into my mouth. Soon, it would begin to overflow, and tiny streams of liquid would trickle down my naked body.

The fact that I allowed Bill to blindfold me was a big step in terms of trust. My hands were free, but I felt extremely vulnerable because I didn't know what he might do. Come to think of it, that's probably one of the things that made it so exciting—not knowing what might happen next.

Bill loved the idea of being the one controlling the fantasy, but he also liked to switch roles and have me control the fantasy. To this day, I'm not quite certain if he liked the dominant or passive role better.

One night Bill asked if I would let him tie me to the bed. I wasn't comfortable with that. True, I trusted him more than I trusted any man, but I just couldn't allow myself to give anyone that much physical control over me.

Since I wouldn't let Bill tie me up, he asked if I would be willing to do it to him. Now that was a piece of light S&M I felt I could get into.

I proceeded to pull two white silk scarves from my dresser and tie Bill's hands to the metal bedposts. Once I had him at my mercy, I teased him until he was crazy with excitement. This game turned us both on. But, as always. Bill wanted to take things a step further.

The next time I tied Bill to the bed, he asked me to use a dildo-shaped vibrator on him. It was exciting to see him getting so aroused, and I couldn't wait to untie him so he could use it on me. Which he did.

I was starting to wonder just how far Bill would try to take our sexual experimentation, when he suggested finding another woman for a threesome. I thought I'd made it clear that I would never be into anything like that. But I had already given Bill so much leeway, he probably figured there was no harm in asking. Once Bill saw that I was offended, he apologized for making the suggestion, and never brought up the subject again.

Even though I was quite certain Bill would never consciously try to force me to do anything against my will, our sexual adventures had started to trouble me. Looking back, I believe Bill and I were like drug addicts. But instead of heroin or cocaine, we were addicted to the escalating sexual excitement we were creating.

Oh, well, it's nice to know that at least one of us eventually got over her addiction to sex!

Chapter 8

♦

Portrait of a Risk Junkie

"[Bill Clinton holds the] reckless belief that he can talk anyone into anything (or, more to the point, that he can talk his way out of anything), that he can seduce and abandon, at will and without consequence."
—Joe Klein (AKA Anonymous)

By 1984 I was homesick for Little Rock. I had been on the road with Roy Clark for over a year, and had been appearing in supper clubs throughout the Southwest.

Soon after my return to Arkansas, Bill and I began seeing each other again on a regular basis. Although I had long since given up hope of a permanent relationship, the passion between us had never died down. Our rendezvous were sporadic during the years I was away. Now both of us desperately wanted to make up for lost time.

Bill suggested that I move into the Quapaw Tower, a high rise building located about a mile from the governor's mansion. Bill managed to get over to my new apartment no fewer than three or four times a week, and our lovemaking was more intense than it had ever been before.

Looking back on it now, I realize I would have been far better off had I stayed away from Bill. At the time, though, the passion between us was too much for me to resist.

"What do you have to lose?" I sometimes asked myself. Today, of course, I have the painful answer to that question. But back then,

it seemed it was Bill taking all the risks. After all, he was a prominent political figure—a family man who might one day have to
answer for his indiscretions.

As for me, the stakes didn't seem all that high. How much could
anyone actually care that Gennifer Flowers, an unmarried singer
had an affair with a married man who was known to be ensnared in
a miserable marriage?

Anyhow, I wasn't particularly concerned. All I knew was that
I was free to carry on however I pleased, and it was going to take
more than a bunch of rumors to stop me from pursuing such a
heavy-duty passion. Nevertheless, I sometimes found myself looking in the mirror and asking, "What is making you so incredibly
hot for this guy after all this time?"

Sure, Bill Clinton was far and away the best lover I'd ever had,
and he stimulated my mind as much as he did my body. Beyond
that, the knowledge that he would never truly be mine gave Bill the
irresistible luster of forbidden fruit.

I was certainly old enough to know that sleeping with a married
man is never something to be proud of. But, obviously, Hillary was
willing to turn a blind eye to our affair.

At one point, Bill told me that, after he hung up from talking
with me one night, Hillary walked into the room and asked, "How's
Gennifer?"

Bill considered the question for a second, then said, "Just fine."
And that was the end of that.

Hillary's reasons for putting up with Bill's adultery baffled me
at the time. Maybe she was into women, as Bill's "she's eaten more
pussy than I ever will" remark conveyed. Or maybe Hillary really
was having an affair with Vince Foster or some other man. In retrospect, the best guess is that Bill and Hillary's marriage was—and still
is—essentially a business arrangement.

Whatever Hillary's reasons might have been for tolerating Bill's
infidelities, I reckoned they weren't my concern at the time. Still,

my affair with the then-governor of Arkansas was an open secret. It seemed to me that someone should have been worried about the potential damage to his image and aspirations Bill's adultery could cause.

Truth is, people in Little Rock had been whispering about us ever since we met, yet Bill made little or no attempt to be discreet. On many occasions, he would have his driver pull the state car up to the front door of my apartment building, walk through the lobby, and take the elevator to my second-floor apartment, completely oblivious to certain people in the lobby who were clocking his every move.

You would think a married governor would have at least had enough common sense to ride the elevator to another floor. After all, a number of Bill's aides lived in the same building, and he could have been visiting any one of them. But discretion never was Bill's strong suit.

Bill liked to jog in the morning, and that routine gave him a handy excuse to get out of the mansion without arousing suspicion. He would jog a few miles to my place, and spend a couple of hours making love to me. Afterward his driver would pick him up in front of my building and drop him off a block or two from the governor's mansion.

Bill would then simply jog the rest of the way back to the mansion, where he would show up panting, as if he'd just finished a grueling workout. I could have vouched that he was exercising—but it wasn't the jogging that had left him breathless.

One security guard who was usually on duty in the mornings made it a practice to monitor Bill's movements whenever he came to Quapaw Tower. That security guard couldn't help but notice that the elevator invariably stopped at the second floor. A quick check of building residents told the guard that none of Governor Clinton's aides lived on that floor. However, a certain Miss Gennifer Flowers did reside there.

Before long, another round of gossip started to spread. I was pleasantly surprised when Bill suggested we try to be a bit more discreet.

"Here's what we can do," I suggested. "I'll prop the side exit door open with a newspaper a few minutes before you're due to arrive. Then you can slip in and walk up two short flights of stairs without being seen."

Bill enjoyed this little piece of deception, though it really didn't do much to kill the gossip. That nosy security guard would walk around the building and observe Bill coming in through the side door. Before long, the word had filtered down through the Little Rock grapevine.

There were other hooks for the rumor mongers to hang their hats on. As governor, Bill could no longer travel alone. He always had a security contingent of one or more Arkansas state troopers with him. While he and I were in bed making love, his driver would be waiting for him in an illegal parking space at the front of the building. I told Bill that there had been a number of complaints about that by some of the Quapaw residents, but he just laughed and said, "So what?"

I sometimes wondered if Bill was intentionally courting danger. Could he have actually been trying to get caught in a scandal so he could then try to wangle his way out of it?

Over the years, a mountain of evidence has surfaced to indicate that Bill Clinton is some kind of risk junkie—as well as a sex junkie. At the time, I wasn't in a position to be judgmental, since there was a part of me that was also drawn to danger. Still, I was never in Bill's league when it came to pushing that particular envelope.

On one occasion, Bill hired my band to play at a Saturday afternoon function at the governor's mansion. There were about sixty people at the party and we were playing on an elevated area in the backyard.

I was wearing a flaming-red silk blouse and a short black satin skirt. As I sang, I spotted Hillary socializing with the various guests.

I had only seen Bill's wife a couple of times, and she'd always appeared kind of frumpy. Today was no exception. She was dressed in a conservative, nondescript pants suit.

And there was Bill, gorgeously dressed in a navy suit, white shirt, and a solid-maroon silk tie. I could hardly help but notice that my lover had his eyes trained directly at me. Before long we were seducing one another with our eyes, and it wasn't subtle. People were trying to talk to Bill, but he was so intensely into our visual lovemaking that he hardly noticed.

Talk about forbidden fruit. Hillary was within just a few feet of Bill and me the entire time. All the while I was singing, I was looking straight at Bill. Let me tell you, I was working him over big time with this seduction game, and he was returning the favor.

After our first set, the band took a break and I headed for the little girls' room. When I came out, Bill was waiting. He rushed right over and kissed me. Then he whispered in my ear: "I need you right now. Let's duck into the men's room and have sex."

Believe me, I was more than ready to accommodate him. I would have ripped his clothes off right there and then, if better judgment had not prevailed. I realized that anybody could walk into that men's room while we were in the act. It just wasn't worth the risk—at least not to me. But Bill took hold of my arm and tried to pull me into that bathroom.

"Stop it!" I said. "Have you lost your mind? We can't do this. Not here. Not now."

"What are you worried about?" he pleaded. "Nobody's in there. Let's go in there and have some fun!"

"You are crazy!" I nearly screamed. "Anybody can walk in here at any time. What if Hillary should find out?"

"Ah, you worry too much," he protested. "Believe me, she'll never know."

At that point, I pulled my arm away from him and headed back to the bandstand.

I don't think Hillary knew what had taken place, but she was certainly aware of the intense eye contact her husband and I'd been engaged in all night. And, as I've said, I'm certain that she had known about our affair for years.

As I was walking offstage for my next break, Hillary and I passed within inches of one another. Our eyes met briefly, but she turned quickly and glared straight ahead. I sensed that she wanted to punch out my lights right there, and I could understand her feelings. If our positions had been reversed, God knows what I might have wanted to do to her.

Thinking back on that incident now, I realize that Bill must have a screw loose to consider pulling a stunt like that in the bathroom of the governor's mansion with a crowd of people— including his wife!—lurking nearby.

What if I would have been crazy enough to go along with him? And we had been caught in the act?

For Gennifer Flowers, it would have been extremely embarrassing, but hardly a life-shattering disaster. But for Governor Bill Clinton, getting caught in the men's room of the governor's mansion with his pants down might well have meant the end of an extremely promising political career.

Doesn't it strike you as ironic that it was Gennifer Flowers—a mere nightclub singer—restraining the man who would eventually occupy the most powerful position in the world from creating an obscene public disgrace? What does that say about the psychological makeup of the man who is supposed to set a shining example to the young people of our nation?

Bill Clinton may be a charming man and a brilliant politician. But he is also someone who has behaved in ways that would make me nervous about the ethics and emotional stability of my plumber— much less my president. Let me tell you why I make such a statement.

In the first place, there is the matter of Bill's drug use. There is no question that Bill Clinton has used both marijuana and cocaine. He would sometimes light up a joint when we were together—and he always inhaled.

I was stunned the first time Bill pulled a marijuana cigarette out of his pocket, though I tried not to show it. Among musicians, getting high on grass had long been commonplace, though I personally never cared for it. I'd been around enough not to be shocked when someone lit up.

Unlike people who are running for political office, I can be honest about my past indiscretions. I grew up at a time when few people didn't try marijuana. It sometimes seemed like more people smoked grass than didn't, and Bill was not part of that minority that abstained—not in the 1970s, 1980s, or early 1990s. But that's not the point.

For most of the time we were together, Bill Clinton was the governor of a state in which marijuana was illegal. If for no other reason, he had no business carrying and lighting up joints. Those same state troopers who were driving Bill around would have busted some kid they stopped in a routine traffic check and caught with a marijuana joint in his pocket.

I have to admit that I didn't push these qualms when Bill and I were together. I was far more interested in him as a lover than as the moral leader of my state. At first I was startled by his lack of discretion, though his casual attitude toward marijuana use turned out to be a rather mild example of Bill's bulletproof mentality.

I made it clear to Bill I was not comfortable with anyone using cocaine in my presence, and he respected that. Still, he talked openly about his cocaine use. I recall him telling me about the weird effect cocaine sometimes had on him. One morning, Bill stopped by on one of his jogs, after having snorted cocaine at a party the previous night:

"I got so fucked up on coke at that party," Bill told me. "The damn stuff made my scalp itch so bad, I couldn't stop scratching." Bill went on to say he felt conspicuous because many of the people at that party were heavily opposed to drugs of any kind.

"I was nervous that if I kept up the scratching, someone would realize that there might be something more serious than dandruff causing me a problem."

I came right out and told Bill that I thought his use of cocaine was both wrong and extremely dangerous. Once again, he just shrugged and laughed off my concerns.

It was clear that this was a man who believed he was both above the law and immune to danger, though I suppose that was part of his appeal. Had I suspected the extent of Bill's involvement with drugs—not to speak of his almost incredible sexual promiscuity—I would have been out of that relationship in a New York minute.

Between 1984 and 1989, none of that stuff was troubling me very much. Bill and I were doing just great in our relationship, though, by 1988, a variety of forces had started to pull us apart.

Bill and Hillary were getting more serious about acting on their presidential ambitions, and for a while Bill was viewed as a serious contender for the 1988 Democratic nomination.

"Oh, yes, I'd very much like to do it," Governor Clinton told an interviewer who asked if he intended to run for president. As always, Hillary was standing right by her man. "I don't have any ambition for him," she mused, "other than what he has for himself."

By the early spring of 1988, Bill had raised millions of dollars in campaign contributions and had all the earmarks of a serious candidate.

The Democratic front-runner at the time was Senator Gary Hart of Colorado. In the opinion polls, Hart was beating out Vice President George Bush, the leading Republican in the race. Many knowledgeable observers were calling Hart the odds-on favorite to be the next president. But it was not to be.

Over the next two months, Senator Hart would be barraged by allegations that he was a womanizer. In early May, a story that was first run in the *Miami Herald* and picked up by the national media accused the married Democratic front-runner of carrying on an adulterous relationship with a twenty-nine-year-old Miami woman named Donna Rice.

A variety of sources confirmed that Hart had recently spent a weekend aboard a yacht called *Monkey Business,* sailing to Bimini on an overnight trip with Miss Rice. Then, several tabloid weeklies ran photos of Hart's Bimini trip, including one showing Rice seductively perched on the senator's lap.

Even as Hart was denying the "smoking-gun" evidence, more allegations surfaced that he had recently slept with at least one other woman. Only weeks after being declared the overwhelming favorite, Gary Hart was forced to withdraw from the 1988 race—his hopes of ever being president permanently dashed.

Most people in Little Rock, including yours truly, saw Gary Hart's downfall as Bill Clinton's golden opportunity to achieve his lifelong ambition. Bill had recently told a reporter that money would be "no barrier" to his nomination, and there appeared to be no other clear-cut favorite to succeed Hart.

It did, of course, occur to me that rumors of Bill's and my affair might cast a shadow over his candidacy. I had no ambition to become the next Donna Rice, but I wasn't worried.

Recently Bill had tried to be somewhat more discreet and we'd stopped seeing each other quite so often. Naturally I was hurt. But, in a way, I felt somewhat more free. Maybe this was my chance to find someone to make a life with.

What I didn't know then was that Bill's handlers had compiled a list of all the women the governor had slept with over the years, and were mulling over strategies for defusing any damaging revelations that might surface from what was later to be termed "bimbo eruptions."

At the time, I sensed the Gary Hart scandal had scared the daylights out of Bill, though I wasn't quite sure as to why. When Bill told me he was leaning toward not running, I came right out and asked him if it was because of all that Donna Rice business. "Nah," he shrugged. "I've just decided that the time isn't right."

I now know that, in light of information that has since surfaced about Bill's womanizing, Senator Hart's indiscretions were little more than a Sunday school picnic when compared to Bill's escapades.

Even though I had no reason to suspect the extent of Bill's liaisons, I had to laugh when I heard him tell the national press that he was dropping out of the race to spend more time with his seven-year-old daughter. Furthermore, Bill insisted, he had no fear of scrutiny into his personal life, although he acknowledged that he and Hillary had "thought about it and. . . . debated it a lot."

Bill then admitted that he had developed a strategy for dealing with potentially embarrassing questions about his personal life, but refused to discuss the matter any further, because he was "not a candidate."

"For whatever it's worth," he concluded, "I'd still like to be president. And if I get another chance, I'll be 110 percent."

I respected Bill's desire to follow his star, but I had my own life to think about. In 1989 I met a man named Finis Shelnutt, and there were immediate sparks between us.

Finis was recently divorced and struck me as being quite vulnerable. At the same time, he appeared to be a solid and stable person. Finis was a vice president with the Southtrust Bank of Alabama and ran its investment office in Little Rock.

As Finis and I got to know each other, I felt that he was a man I might marry. This was the first time I'd felt closely involved with anyone in years, and I took those feelings as a signal that the time had come to end my affair with Bill.

Breaking up with Bill was not going to be easy. We had been together for twelve years, and had a deep affection for one another. When Bill and I began our affair, I was only twenty-seven years old. Now, at thirty-nine, I realized that it was time to take an honest look at our relationship and where my life was going.

As much as I loved the guy and believed he loved me, I knew I would never be more than his outside woman. As excruciating as it was, I decided what had to be done.

It was a Tuesday night. Bill dropped in, and we immediately began to make love. I had resolved this would be the last time. Once in his arms, though, I could feel myself weakening.

How could I give this up? This was the man I had been closer to than any other. We had known each other so well and had shared so many wonderful memories. Did I really have the strength to let it end?

After we'd gotten dressed, Bill and I sat on the couch and started talking. Suddenly I pulled him to me and whispered, "Darling, it's over. We can't be lovers anymore."

Bill's face was flush. "Uh, can we talk about it?" he stammered.

I got right to the point. Told him that I'd met someone I felt I could make a life with. "As long as you and I are together," I added, "how can I possibly devote myself to anyone else? No, I'm afraid it has to end right here."

Bill was silent for a moment, then tears began to roll down his face. Like me, he could hardly believe the end had come at last. I could see him choking back his heartbreak as he whispered, "I understand, and I want you to do what you need to do for your life."

That was more than I could take. I burst into tears too, and we had our last cry together. Bill Clinton had been the major focus of my life for so long, and severing the bond between us was one of the hardest things I've ever had to do.

As Bill walked to the door, he turned to me and said softly, "If you ever change your mind and want me to come back, all you have to do is call me." I nodded and touched his hand. As he was walking out, he pleaded, "At least, let's keep in touch. Please, let's talk."

Bill and I did remain good friends for the next two years. Then events started spinning out of control, and we became the lead players in one of the most high-profile scandals in the history of American presidential politics.

Chapter 9

♦

The Long Goodbye

"You gotta figure he ain't gonna get caught like [Gary] Hart. Some bimbo from a former life comes forward, and we just say–Bullshit."
—from *Primary Colors* by Anonymous

Bill and I did stay in touch after our love affair ended. Even though our contact was limited to phone conversations, we remained close friends—or at least that's what I thought at the time.

I couldn't imagine cutting off all communication with my lover of twelve years, and I was always happy to hear from him. Bill seemed to be getting his life in order and moving forward with his political plans. We talked about a lot of things, but inevitably he would try to convince me that we should get back together.

"No way," I would tell him. Finis and I were becoming increasingly close, and I wasn't about to jeopardize that relationship. Bill always said he understood. But the next time he called, he would again try to convince me to change my mind.

Several months after Bill and I broke up, Finis and I went to the horse races in Hot Springs. Shortly after we sat down, I spotted Bill. It was the first time I had seen him since our final night together.

After a while, Finis went to get us something to drink, and I found myself sitting alone in our box. A few minutes later, Bill came over and sat down next to me.

People were staring, but, as usual, Bill couldn't have cared less. However, I was relieved that Finis wasn't around to see the longing in Bill's eyes. I still hadn't told Finis about my relationship with Bill, and didn't want to broach the subject at that point.

Bill only visited with me for a few minutes, and we had a nice, friendly conversation. As Bill left, he flashed a wistful smile. Finis returned several minutes later, unaware of what had just taken place.

By now, it was 1990, and Bill's final reelection campaign for governor of Arkansas was in full swing. During the last stages of that campaign, a former state employee, Larry Nichols, filed a lawsuit against Bill for defamation of character. It is my understanding that Bill fired Nichols because of allegations that Nichols was making unauthorized long-distance telephone calls. In retaliation, Nichols filed a lawsuit charging Bill with using state funds to finance a number of adulterous affairs.

Nichols's lawsuit referred to several unnamed women, but five women—including me—were specifically identified. I knew nothing about the lawsuit until Finis called to tell me that a press release about the Nichols lawsuit was faxed to his office, and that my name was among those mentioned.

Even though I hadn't told Finis about my affair with Bill, he may have suspected it. Still, rumors are one thing. Having your name smeared all over town as one of the governor's many mistresses is quite another.

Finis and I had been seeing each other for almost a year, and we had gotten very close. Now I could see it all destroyed, and I was in tears when Finis came over to talk about it.

To my great relief, Finis never asked me if there was any basis to the rumors. Instead, he sensed my dismay and tried hard to comfort me. I was grateful for the restraint and empathy Finis showed, but I knew deep down that these revelations would ultimately destroy our relationship.

As awful as I felt about Finis, there was an even more troubling side to the Nichols assertions. If Bill was as promiscuous as the lawsuit had claimed, I had been played for a fool. Not only that, my life had been put at risk.

When Bill and I first started sleeping together, nobody had even heard of AIDS. But we were now into the 1990s, and I was mortified by thoughts of the grave danger Bill's alleged womanizing may have exposed me to.

Bill had never used a condom when we made love, and I never asked him to. I thought the only thing I had to worry about was birth control. Suddenly I realized how foolish I might have been.

When I first saw the list of women named in Larry Nichols's lawsuit, there was only one I suspected might have had an affair with Bill—Deborah Mathis, who had worked with me as a reporter at KARK-TV. Deborah was an attractive, sexy woman who'd spent a lot of time with Bill in her capacity as a reporter. I recalled that early in our relationship, Bill had cautioned me about getting too chummy with her.

My first instinct was to call Bill and discuss the matter with him, but suddenly my thoughts started running in another direction. In the past I had trusted Bill implicitly. Now I wondered if he was capable of lying to me about his other affairs—and anything else—to further his master plan. Still, I did want to see what he'd have to say about these charges, so we discussed it over the phone. Predictably, Bill went down the names and explained them all away. All except Deborah.

I decided not to push the matter with Bill at that point, but I was devastated. For the first time, I started thinking about how exposed Bill had left me. If those allegations about other women were true, he had certainly endangered my health.

In time, more rumors of Bill's womanizing would surface, and I would eventually get myself tested for AIDS. Thank goodness I was found to be free of HIV infection and all other sexually transmitted diseases. But that didn't soothe my anger at Bill for so

casually leaving me open to that kind of danger. And it made
me wonder:

What other lies had he told me in the past?

What other dangers might he expose me to in the future?

A number of friends had advised me to tape my telephone conversations with Bill, just in case I ever needed to substantiate the
nature of our relationship. I had always laughed off such sugges-
tions. This was a man I had loved and cherished. I felt positive that
he would never hurt me. Now I wasn't so sure.

I started recalling all the rumors I'd heard over the years about
what happened to people who tried to cross or who became a threat
to Bill Clinton. I had sometimes broached these questions with Bill
when we were together, but he always sloughed them off. Now, suddenly I was frightened. What if Bill and his people began viewing
me as a threat? Maybe it wouldn't be such a bad idea to take my
friends' advice.

I had a little tape recorder that I used when I finalized verbal
contracts over the phone for singing engagements. Over the coming
months, I would wind up taping four of my phone conversations
with Bill. Still, I didn't feel all that wonderful about taping him
without his knowledge.

Bill and I would still talk fairly often, but I had started to sense
things that caused me to believe that, at some point, events might
start to spin out of control. In that case, I really would need to
protect myself.

Whatever fears I might have been harboring, it never crossed
my mind that my ex-lover wanted to stay on my good side as part of
a preconceived damage-control strategy. It now appears that this is
exactly what he was trying to do.

After what had happened to Gary Hart's candidacy in 1988, the
Clintons must have known that the press would come to Arkansas
looking for any dirt they could dig up. The American people might
not care much about a corrupt, womanizing governor of some tiny
backwater state. But Bill Clinton was now shaping up to be a

serious presidential candidate, and any scandals concerning him would make national headlines.

How would Bill respond when the inevitable questions were asked about his adultery? The Clinton spin team had four years to help Bill learn his lines. I can imagine the kind of advice they gave him behind closed doors.

"Don't get too defensive."

"Speak with confidence—as if you have right on your side."

"Don't respond directly to any specific charges."

"Admit that you've had problems in your marriage—as many other couples do—but add that you've gotten beyond them."

It was, of course, at least as important that Hillary have her lines down when the fur started to fly. Gary Hart's wife Lee had acted defensive in the wake of allegations of her husband's womanizing. Hillary was not about to fall into that trap. As always, she would be the strong one—the steadfast power behind a wobbly throne.

But what would happen if one or more of Bill's outside women came forward? No problem, the Clinton team figured. After all, who were these bimbos? Nobodies. Flies on the wall who could be neutralized by paid spin merchants or intimidated into silence by threats.

If all else failed, Bill would resort to that old hocus pocus of asking: "Who do you believe, me or your lying eyes?" In other words, he would deny everything no matter how damning the evidence. Not only that, he would find ways to induce others to support those lies. As he noted in one of our taped phone conversations:

"If they ever hit you with [charges that we had an affair], just say no and go on. There's nothing they can do . . . if everybody kind of hangs tough, they're just not going to do anything."

What Bill seemed most worried about was that some incriminating photograph of him and me surface. He felt that Senator Hart might have weathered the storm if someone hadn't produced photos of him and Donna Rice.

Over the years, there had been lots of talk about photos. There was Gary Johnson, that next door neighbor of mine in Quapaw Tower who claimed to have a videotape of Bill walking into my apartment. As I mentioned, someone broke into Johnson's apartment and beat the poor guy to a pulp. After that, nobody ever heard another word about incriminating videotapes.

I recently read that a photograph exists showing Bill getting into a car driven by me, but I have no direct knowledge of this or any other such photo. I hope that helps Bill and his spin team breathe a little easier.

There have been all sorts of phone records and other written and verbal documentation showing Bill cavorting with me and other women, but the only thing that seems to worry him is visual evidence. Some Clinton advisors have talked about his "almost mystical faith in the absence of photographs." This is confirmed by some of the things he said in our taped conversations.

In one of the conversations, I ask Bill if he intended to run for president.

"I want to [run for president]," he answered. "I wonder if I'm just going to be blown out of the water with [these allegations of womanizing]. I don't see how they can [have overlooked it] so far."

"I don't think they can," I replied.

"Oh, they don't, if they don't have pictures," Bill then said. "Which they [can't have of] anybody, and [if] no one says anything. Then they don't have anything. And, arguably, if someone says something, they [still] don't have much."

Personally, I don't really see why a photograph would necessarily be any more valid proof than some of the things he said on our tape-recorded conversations. I have no doubt, though, that Bill's spin team would move heaven and earth to squelch or discredit a photograph or any other piece of evidence. And they would have no qualms about destroying the person who produced it.

During the summer of 1990, my mother was diagnosed with cancer, and was going through a year-long course of chemotherapy and radiation treatments. Thank goodness those treatments made her cancer-free. During the time of her ordeal, I was trying to spend as much time as possible with my mother. But the entertainment industry was drying up in Little Rock, and it looked as though I would have to move.

I knew that my chances of finding singing work would be better in any number of other cities, but I wanted to be close to my mother during this crisis. That meant I had to find a way to stay in Little Rock.

I figured that, if I had a steady job, I would be able to remain in Little Rock, be near Mother, and sing on weekends to supplement my income. I called Bill, explained the situation, and asked if he could help me get a state job. He expressed concern about my mother's health and said he was quite certain that something could be done for me in the way of a job.

So there you have it. Governor Bill Clinton was instrumental in getting Gennifer Flowers a modest state job. Is there any politician—Democrat or Republican—who hasn't done much heavier favors for friends and relatives? Of course, no politician will ever admit to engaging in patronage. But anybody with two good eyes and half a brain ought to know what's going on.

Look at the people Bill Clinton has appointed to key federal positions, including some in the White House. They are largely long-time friends of his and Hillary's. Is there something wrong with hiring your friends? Maybe so, but this is a practice far more pervasive even than college students smoking marijuana in the 1970s.

There's no question that my name was pushed ahead of others on the list. Still, I was overqualified for that administrative assistant's position. The fix may have been in, but I did not lie about attending college, as has been alleged.

I would like to believe that Bill helped me get the state job because he cared about me as a friend—not simply to shut me up. I'm not so sure anymore. Nevertheless, the thought has occurred to me: If Bill really feared that I would sell my story for big bucks, why would he think a low-paying clerical position would keep my lips sealed?

A woman who I once let stay with me in Dallas has said any number of unflattering things about me to the press. But even she was purported to have made the following statement:

"I've tried to tell Gennifer for years that she should come out with the story, but she didn't want to wreck [Bill Clinton's] career."

For once, this person had it right. The last thing on my mind was joining a lynch party whose goal it was to bring Bill Clinton down. I wished him well in realizing his dream, and had no intention of going public with our affair—much less cashing in on it.

When the story of Bill's womanizing first hit the national press, I tried in vain to hide from the media. By then, my apartment had been illegally entered three times and my life had been threatened. To my great disappointment, Bill had totally distanced himself from me. What's worse, I had suspected that Bill's operatives may have been behind some of those attempts to intimidate me into keeping my mouth shut.

There I was, frightened and alone. Nevertheless, had Bill made any attempt to explain himself or help me during that trying time, I never would have shared our private moments with the public.

When reporters from the *Star* approached me, they made it clear that they were going to write about my romance with Bill, with or without my cooperation. They then offered me a substantial amount of money for my participation, and I reluctantly agreed.

Let me again emphasize that I did not seek out the press and offer my story for money, but I was in a tough spot. It was clear that both my singing career in Little Rock and the state government job were dead issues as a result of the notoriety the *Star* story would cause. I was going to have to relocate and, since the story was going to be published anyway, I decided to cooperate with the magazine.

Now I ask you: Does the fact that I took money for corroborating events that actually took place in my life automatically compromise my credibility?

If so, what can we say about the credibility of certain politicians and media professionals who are well compensated for defending certain people and points of view? How should we evaluate the credibility of Bill and Hillary Clinton, who have the resources to hire paid apologists to deflect charges and allegations that pose a threat to their overreaching ambitions?

When the *Star* story first appeared, the Clintons had agreed to go on *Nightline* to refute them. Instead of showing up, they sent a hired gun who was specifically retained to refute those accusations.

That hit woman was 34-year-old Mandy Grunwald, a gangly, Harvard-educated, Marlboro-smoking media consultant. Grunwald comes from a wealthy New York family, and fancies herself a populist whose interests lie with helping the little people. The perfect kind of gal to fight Bill and Hillary's battles.

Grunwald asked Ted Koppel why he hadn't talked about Bill Clinton's social and economic programs. Why, she pointedly asked, was he "making this program about some unsubstantiated charges that . . . started with a trashy supermarket tabloid?"

Ted Koppel then responded by saying: "You've done a very effective job of putting [me] on the defensive. . . . That's what you're here to do. But the question is whether a story like this deserves to be told. . . . You are an adviser to this particular candidate. Let me ask you: If he asked your personal advice, and maybe he did, would you have told him to come on *Nightline* tonight and confront it? Or would you tell him to ignore it?"

Grunwald then responded, "I'm not an adviser to Governor Clinton. My partner is."

Many people felt Grunwald had rattled the normally unflappable *Nightline* host. You've got to hand it to the Clintons—sending a female consultant who wasn't yet an official part of the team, one who could sit there with a straight face and ask the public to believe that she was not a hired gun, but rather a private citizen concerned only with truth and ethics.

In recruiting Grunwald, Bill and Hillary must have talked about the stark contrast she would pose to the woman they had painted as a money-hungry bimbo. What could be better than a bookwormish "idealist" who goes on TV, not for the money, but because she sincerely believes in what she is talking about?

Sorry to shatter your illusions, folks, but less than twenty-four hours after that impressive *Nightline* performance, the Clintons put Mandy Grunwald on their payroll. Before long, she was in charge of media and advertising.

Oh, well, let's not be too hard on Ms. Grunwald and others who receive big bucks fronting for the Clintons. Everybody's entitled to make a living, aren't they? Even Bill and Hillary Clinton—those paragons of virtue who want us to believe that they care only about the welfare of the little people they serve.

It appears that the so-called little people Bill and Hillary are so concerned about are facing an uncertain future. But the president and his family can rest easy about their financial fortunes. They will have it made no matter how well or poorly Bill's tenure in office is judged.

You may have noticed that even the nearly impeached Richard Nixon wasn't excluded from the lush world of seven-figure book deals and six-figure speaking engagements. So let's not worry about old Bill. He and his kin are going to do just fine—however tilted the playing field may be for the rest of us. And once those fat bucks come rolling in, Bill and Hillary are sure to find ever so resourceful ways to shelter their money.

Meanwhile, the money I received from the *Star* is long gone. Like you, I continue to work hard to achieve my goals. I continue to perform my cabaret act, both here and abroad, and have been approached to host my own radio talkshow. So please don't get sidetracked by all this garbage about my credibility being called into question because I received some money. Read and listen to Bill Clinton's own words in our taped phone conversations. Then consider those in light of the many new revelations that paint an even more troubling picture of the man.

When the Troopergate scandal broke in 1994, several Arkansas state troopers who had served as Governor Clinton's drivers and bodyguards confirmed widespread rumors of Bill's incredibly promiscuous behavior with women. These include more recent allegations by several of the troopers that Bill:

- Hit on several wives and daughters of his most well-heeled political backers.
- Attempted to have sex with a woman in the playground of Chelsea's school.
- Slipped a woman wearing a trenchcoat into the basement of the governor's mansion for sex, six days before he was inaugurated President, while Hillary and Chelsea were asleep upstairs.

What do you think? Should we tolerate this kind of behavior from our president, or just laugh it off? After all, Bill Clinton isn't the first guy in the White House to have sex with someone other than his wife. George Washington and Thomas Jefferson were both well-known dabblers in the romantic arts. FDR had an ongoing affair, and JFK's womanizing was legendary. Some say that Lyndon Johnson was the most outrageous rogue of all—and even Jimmy Carter has admitted to having sinned in his mind.

So now we have this young, sexy, good-looking guy in the White House. He's obviously stuck in a crummy marriage and has an overactive sexual appetite. Why shouldn't we give the boy some slack? If he wants to go out and get his ashes hauled, why not let him?

Lord knows, I'm no saint. And as far as I'm concerned, Bill Clinton, *the man*, can do anything he pleases—now that he no longer shares my bed. Still, it seems to me that this president's sexual promiscuity is about a lot more than who he is screwing. It goes to the very heart of who he is.

I have always believed that we need a person in the White House whose character is beyond reproach, and I'm not about to revise that opinion. As journalist Joe Klein, a supporter of Bill Clinton, has written in a *Newsweek* article aptly titled "The Politics of Promiscuity":

"This president's charm is a tantalizing attribute. He has other endearing qualities as well, including a good heart and some admirable goals—all of which suggest, when he's at his best, a potential for greatness. But greatness isn't possible without a steadfast character. It's not too much to ask that a leader be mature, fully formed and not flailing about in a narcissistic, existential quest for self-discovery. Life may be a journey; but character, most assuredly, is not. . . . It is both tragic and quite dangerous that we find ourselves still asking if Bill Clinton will ever get there."

Klein points out that President Clinton's "promiscuity" is a threat to his effectiveness. And some whose job it is to guard the president's life also worry about the danger it poses to national security. Gary Aldrich, a former FBI agent who worked in the White House during both the Bush and Clinton administrations, has added to Bill's legacy of womanizing and edgy behavior:

"I have been informed by a well-placed White House source that there are times when the president, the leader of the free world, is missing—that is, cannot be located by staff—for hours at a time. . . .

"The Secret Service should know where the president is at all times. But this is no longer the case, I have been informed, because the first lady has booted them out of the Residence. Moreover, she does not always know where the president is, because the Clintons sleep in separate bedrooms."

Aldrich then asks the next logical question: "If the president cannot be found, where is he?"

Aldrich alleges that the president is "a frequent late-night visitor to the Marriott Hotel in downtown Washington, which has an underground parking garage with an elevator that allows guests to go to their rooms without passing through the lobby."

According to Aldrich's sources, the room is booked by a woman, whom the president meets by literally sneaking out of the White House gate without any security.

"The president's driver is believed to be Bruce Lindsey, a

high-level White House staffer and longtime friend of the president. The car is parked near the elevator. The driver waits in the car until the president returns, often hours later. The car usually arrives after midnight and sometimes leaves early in the morning, sometimes as late as 4:00 A.M."

To a security-conscious FBI man like Gary Aldrich, the president's traveling to these trysts unprotected is the issue of major concern, and I think he has a good point. To me, Bill's behavior is reminiscent of a child who needs to test the limits in order to see just how much he can get away with. The question is: Can the rest of us afford the potential consequences of finding out how much is too much? I believe Joe Klein answers that question quite nicely in "The Politics of Promiscuity":

"The president has told members of his inner circle, 'Character is a journey, not a destination.' This is . . . a matter of personal experience: in the president's life, displays of character have usually involved perseverance rather than principle. . . . But this evolutionary notion of character is also something of a finesse: it can drift from explaining lapses to excusing them. There is an adolescent, unformed, half-baked quality to it. . . . It will not suffice in a president."

Whatever I may think about Bill Clinton as president, a part of me will always care for him as a person, and I believe in my heart that he will always care for me.

Sometimes I wonder: Is it healthy to confront these demons from a past that is still very much with me? I have tried to go on with my life, but it hasn't been easy. I fear that I will always remain a marked woman to those who seek to use me as a symbol to further their own ends, but I need to get on with my own life—haunted though it may be.

Deep down, I know that part of me will never be able to say goodbye to my passionate years with Bill Clinton. My heart aches for both of us, and all the might-have-beens that never were.

I don't know what the future holds for me or my lost lover. All I know is that he is stuck in a loveless marriage, and I haven't yet succeeded in finding a permanent relationship with a man. Whatever happens, nothing and nobody can ever take away the wonderful times we shared.

If I thought my letter would get through his White House screeners, here is what I would write:

Dearest Bill:

You and I have somehow become pitted against one another. I doubt that we will ever come face-to-face again. Even if we do, you'll probably have to pretend I'm not there. That's okay. You will always have an important place in my heart. And, darling, I am quite sure I will have a special place in yours.

Love,
Gennifer

Chapter 10

♦

Living Proof

"They can't run a story like this unless somebody said, 'Yeah, I did it with him.'"

—Bill Clinton

As this book goes to press, Bill Clinton has still never acknowledged the nature of our relationship, but my taped conversations with him reveal where the truth lies. There were four taped conversations, recorded between December 1990 and January 1992. The voices on those tapes (Bill's and mine) were authenticated by computer-certified tests conducted by Truth Verification Laboratories in White Plains, New York.

The excerpts that follow were played at a press conference on January 28, 1992, the day my story appeared in the *Star*. On the previous night, Bill and Hillary Clinton had appeared on *60 Minutes* to refute my story. Here is my opening statement to the press, and a transcript of the taped excerpts they heard.

Good afternoon. This whole experience is not easy for me. I will start by explaining why I came forward to tell my story about my affair with Governor Bill Clinton. I quite simply was afraid. Afraid I'd be out on the street without a job. I had already started to lose singing engagements

because of the rumors about Bill and me, and I thought I'd
lose my state job Bill helped me get. The pressure was so
intense, I thought I might have to leave Little Rock, which
is my home.

In 1990 Larry Nichols had filed a lawsuit naming me as
one of Bill's lovers. The rumor spread and the pressure was
enormous. I was scared and I was alone. To protect myself I
began taping my telephone conversations.

The situation was snowballing and I didn't know what
was going to happen next. I wanted to have a record of the
relationship. Then things got out of control. First I heard
that *Star* was going to run a story about Larry Nichols's
lawsuit. When I heard Bill describe our relationship as an
absolute, total lie, I knew what my decision should be. To
tell my side of the story truthfully, and as quickly as possible. So I'm here to repeat, in front of all of you, what I
said in my *Star* article.

Yes, I was Bill Clinton's lover for twelve years, and for
the past two years I have lied to the press about our relationship to protect him. The truth is, I loved him. Now he tells
me to deny it. Well, I'm sick of all the deceit, and I'm sick of
all the lies. Last night I sat and watched Bill on *60 Minutes*.
I felt disgusted and I saw a side of Bill that I had never seen
before. He is absolutely lying. I'm disappointed, but realisti-
cally I never thought he would come out and admit it. When
people hear my tapes, I think they will realize that I am not
a woman that he saw and spoke to infrequently.

My tapes go far beyond what Bill described last evening
[on *60 Minutes*]. He described our relationship as a friendly
acquaintance that was very limited—friendly, but limited.
Listen to the tape excerpts, then judge for yourself if this
is the way a man talks to a woman who is just a friendly
acquaintance.

There were two conversations in the tapes that embarrass me now, but remember, I was talking to a man I had loved for twelve years. I feel confident about my story because I'm telling the truth. The man on *60 Minutes* was not the man I fell in love with. I've dealt with my hurt for two years now, so this is nothing new to me. I would have liked to think that after a twelve-year relationship he would have had the guts to say, "Yes, I had an affair with this woman, but it's over. And that's the truth."

Thank you.

The first two excerpts are from two tape recordings made between September and December of 1991. You will note that in a number of instances, Bill Clinton asks me to lie on his behalf about, among other things, our relationship, and regarding his role in helping me get a state job.

Please note that, in the following excerpts, the ellipses (. . .) are used to indicate vocal pauses and trailing off of phrases—so as to give the flavor of the actual conversation. In some instances, there are words added for the purpose of clarifying missing or garbled bits of conversation. These are indicated by notes within brackets [ ].

Tape segment 1

G. FLOWERS. Are you there? Sorry about that. Mother was . . . wanted me to get her a glass of water. See, that was another thing. See, my parents are here, and I'll tell you what, the last thing I needed was to. . . .

B. CLINTON. Have that happen. . . .

G. FLOWERS. Have that happen, 'cause my mother would get very concerned and worried, and so far, you know. . . .

B. CLINTON. [garbled] If they ever hit you with it just say no and go on. There's nothing they can do.

G. FLOWERS. Well, I will, but I mean . . . I . . . you know . . . she's my mother and you know how mothers can be.

B. CLINTON. They don't want to hear it at all.

G. FLOWERS. Well, she would just get all in a tizzy about . . . about it and uh, so I thought, "Good God, that's all I need." 'Cause they're, uh, they're gonna be here . . . well, they're leaving Wednesday morning and they were at the club tonight and they'll be here tomorrow night, which, you know, parents do. And I thought, "Oh, please, Jesus, don't let those people [the press] be out there."

B. CLINTON. I'm just sorry that you ever had to put up with that [next word is garbled].

G. FLOWERS. Well, you know, to be real honest with you, I'm not completely surprised. I didn't think it would start this quickly. But I think, Bill, you're being naive if you think that these other shows like *Current Affair* and, oh, what are some of the others? Uh. . . .

B. CLINTON. Well, I thought they. . . .

G. FLOWERS. *Hard Copy.*

B. CLINTON. I thought they'd look into it. But, you know, I just think a crazy person like Larry Nichols is not enough to get a story on the television with names in it.

G. FLOWERS. Right. Well, he better not get on there and start naming names.

B. CLINTON. Well, that's what I mean. You know, if all the people who are named . . . deny it. . . . that's all. I mean, I expect them to come look into it and interview you and everything, uh, but I just think that if everybody's on record denying it you've got no problem.

G. FLOWERS. Well, I don't think . . . I don't think it . . . I don't . . . Well, why would they waste their money and time coming down here unless someone showed 'em some interest? See, they weren't here tonight and they're not going to be there.

B. CLINTON. No, no. See, that's it. I mean, they're gonna run this Larry Nichols thing down. They're gonna try to goad people up, you know. But if everybody kinda hangs tough, they're just not going to do anything. They can't.

G. FLOWERS. No. They can't.

B. CLINTON. They can't run a story like this unless somebody said, "Yeah, I did it with him."

B. CLINTON. I'll tell you what, it would be extremely valuable if they ever do run anybody by me, you know. If they ever get anybody to do this, just to have, like I told you before when I called you, is to have an on-file affidavit explaining that, you know, you were approached by a Republican and asked to do that.

G. FLOWERS. Mm hmm. Well. . . .

B. CLINTON. [garbled] . . . the more I think about it, you should call him back. . . . [garbled] just don't know.

G. FLOWERS. Well, I think that . . . Well, are you going to run? [laughs] Can you tell me that?

B. CLINTON. I want to. I wonder if I'm going to be blown out of the water with this. I don't see how they can [garbled word] so far.

G. FLOWERS. I don't think they can. . . .

B. CLINTON. If they don't, if they don't have pictures. . . .

G. FLOWERS. Mm hmm.

B. CLINTON. Which they [don't]. And if . . . and no one says anything, then they don't have anything and, arguably, if someone says something, they don't have much.

G. FLOWERS. If they could blow you out of the water they would have already blown you. I really believe that because I believe that there are various ones that have been trying hard lately. See, like that *Inside Edition*. Uh—there've probably been other sources too. [Pause] So . . . I don't think so. I honestly don't. That's my gut feeling. I would tell you if I did. [pause] But . . . you may know more about. . . .

B. CLINTON. How do you like holding [my] . . . future in . . . [your] hands? . . . Do you like that?

G. FLOWERS. Yeah. [laughs] No. Well, if it's positive I do, you know. I mean 'cause I want you to . . . I would love to see you

go. . . . Oh, I'd love to see you be president. I think that would
be wonderful. I think you'd make a . . . damn good one. I don't
like Bush. I think he's a sneaky bastard. [laughs] [garbled] He's
two-faced. I'd just love to see somebody get in there for a change,
really make a difference. But, uh . . . It's like I told you before,
whatever you need me to do, just let me know.

B. CLINTON. I will.

Tape segment 2

G. FLOWERS. Remember a long time ago when you called me and
   said that if you announced for—well, it was back the first time
   you were going to announce for, uh. . . .

B. CLINTON. Governor?

G. FLOWERS. No. President. [laughs] [garbled] And you said
   [garbled] "Gennifer, [I] just wanted you to know that there might
   be some reporters or something out there," and you said, "Now,
   uh, you be sure to [garbled words] [both laugh] say 'There's
   nothing to the rumor,' and I said, okay. I, well, I shouldn't even
   say this to you—probably embarrass you. Do you remember what
   I said to you?

B. CLINTON. No. What'd you say?

G. FLOWERS. I said—well, at the time, "You eat good pussy." [laughs]

B. CLINTON. What?

G. FLOWERS. I said I had to tell them that you ate good pussy and
   you said, "Well you can tell them that if I don't run for President." [laughs] I've got to keep my voice down. My parents are
   in the other . . . [laughs] [garbled]

B. CLINTON. [garbled]

G. FLOWERS. And I thought, you know, that's not real funny right
   now. But, anyway, I try to find the humor in things.

B. CLINTON. Don't I know it. [garbled] [garbled]

G. FLOWERS. Well, I can guarantee you that's not something I've
   thought about [laughs]. That's not the first thing on my mind
   when I think about those reporters being down there.

B. CLINTON. God.

G. FLOWERS. Oh, Lord.

B. CLINTON. [garbled]

G. FLOWERS. But, anyway, I think we're okay for now.

B. CLINTON. [garbled] . . . we have to watch as we go along.

G. FLOWERS. Well, you're, uh, you know—from the feedback I'm getting around me about various things that are going on with what you're doing, I'm getting very positive feedback.

B. CLINTON. Yeah, there's no negative except this.

G. FLOWERS. This is the only thing.

B. CLINTON. And there's no negative to me running except this and, even if I win . . . as a matter of fact it might be better for me to lose the primary. I might lose the nomination to Bob Kerrey because he's um . . . got all the Gary Hart/Hollywood money and because he's single, looks like a movie star, won the Medal of Honor, and since he's single, nobody cares if he's screwing [laughs].

These next two excerpts are from a conversation that took place on December 16, 1992. Bill was phoning from Washington, D.C., the night before he was scheduled to participate in the first TV debate with his five rivals for the Democratic Party presidential candidacy. In these conversations, you can hear him asking me to lie about his role in helping me get a state job.

Tape segment 3

(Phone rings)

G. FLOWERS. Hello?

B. CLINTON. Gennifer?

G. FLOWERS. Yes.

B. CLINTON. It's Bill Clinton.

G. FLOWERS. Hi, Bill.

B. CLINTON. Hey, I tried to call you. I can't believe I got you.

G. FLOWERS. Well, when did you try to call me?

B. CLINTON. Last night. Late.

G. FLOWERS. Well, I was here.

B. CLINTON. Did you take your phone off the hook?

G. FLOWERS. Well, I did. Well, I've been getting these hang-up calls.

B. CLINTON. Oh.

G. FLOWERS. And at one point I took my phone. . . . I, well, I didn't take it off the hook, I just, uh. . . .

B. CLINTON. Turned it off?

G. FLOWERS. Yeah.

B. CLINTON. Oh, that's what it was. I called . . . I started calling soon as I got home last night and I called for a couple of hours.

G. FLOWERS. Well, sorry I missed you.

B. CLINTON. [garbled] . . . I was afraid I screwed up the number or something, and I kept calling.

G. FLOWERS. Well, are you . . . you got a cold?

B. CLINTON. Yeah. Oh, it's just my . . . every year about this time, my sinuses go bananas.

G. FLOWERS. Yeah, me too.

B. CLINTON. And I've been in this stupid airplane too much, but I'm okay.

G. FLOWERS. Well, good. Good. The reason I was calling was to tell you that, uh, well—a couple things. Uh, this last Wednesday, someone got into my apartment.

B. CLINTON. Hold on a minute.

G. FLOWERS. Okay.

[long pause]

B. CLINTON. Okay, I got it.

G. FLOWERS. Are you in Little Rock?

B. CLINTON. No.

G. FLOWERS. No.

B. CLINTON. I am going to be there tonight late. I'm in, uh, Washington now and. . . .

G. FLOWERS. Well. . . .

B. CLINTON. I'm going to Dallas, and then I'm coming to Little Rock.

G. FLOWERS. Uh, well. . . .

B. CLINTON. So somebody broke in your apartment?

G. FLOWERS. Well, yeah, well . . . There wasn't any sign of a break-in, uh, but the drawers and things . . . There wasn't anything missing that I can tell but somebody had. . . .

B. CLINTON. Somebody had gone through all your stuff?

G. FLOWERS. And gone through my stuff.

B. CLINTON. You think they were. . . . But they didn't steal anything?

G. FLOWERS. No. No, my jewelry . . . I had jewelry here and everything, it was still here.

B. CLINTON. You think they were trying to look for something on us?

G. FLOWERS. I think so. Well, I mean . . . why. . . why else? Um. . . .

B. CLINTON. You weren't missing any kind of papers or anything?

G. FLOWERS. Well, like what kind of papers?

B. CLINTON. Well, I mean, did . . . any kind of personal records or checkbooks or anything like that? . . . Phone records?

G. FLOWERS. Do I have any?

B. CLINTON. Yeah.

G. FLOWERS. Unh unh. I mean, why would I?

B. CLINTON. I don't know I just. . . .

G. FLOWERS. You . . . you usually call me, for that matter. And besides, who would know?

B. CLINTON. Isn't that amazing?

G. FLOWERS. Even if I had it on my phone record. . . . Oh, well, I guess they might be able to say, "Oh, well, you were in Washington on this date and maybe at that number," and connect that but. . . .

B. CLINTON. Well. . . .

G. FLOWERS. See, you've always called me. So that's not a. . . .

B. CLINTON. I wouldn't care if they . . . you know, I . . . They may have my phone records on this computer here, but I don't think it. . . . That doesn't prove anything.

G. FLOWERS. Well, that . . . that's true. But I just want to tell you about that.

B. CLINTON. Wow.

G. FLOWERS. Let me tell you something positive.

B. CLINTON. What?

G. FLOWERS. Uh, I heard, uh . . . I've heard a couple of people say—one had been to San Antonio, the other had been to Los Angeles . . . and they both said that they were, uh, that all they heard out there was, "Clinton, Clinton, Clinton," so. . . .

B. CLINTON. Really?

G. FLOWERS. Yeah. So I thought that was exciting.

B. CLINTON. We've worked so hard.

G. FLOWERS. I know you have, but I . . . That may not be a lot, but I mean, that's a . . . I think that's a good indication.

B. CLINTON. Well, no, no. . . . Most people think, you know, that, except for Cuomo, I'm doing the best right now and, uh. . . . We're leading in the polls in Florida . . . without Cuomo in there, but Cuomo's at eighty-seven percent name recognition, and I have fifty-four percent, so . . . I mean . . . I'm at a terrible disadvantage in name recognition still, but we're coming up, and . . . so I . . .We're moving pretty well, I'm really pleased about it.

G. FLOWERS. Well, I don't particularly care for Cuomo's demeanor.

B. CLINTON. Boy, he is so aggressive.

G. FLOWERS. Well, he seems like he could get real mean [laughs].

B. ClINTON. [garbled]

G. FLOWERS. Yeah . . . I wouldn't be surprised if he didn't have some Mafioso major connections.

B. CLINTON. Well he acts like one [laughs].

G. FLOWERS. Yeah.

♦

Tape segment 4

G. FLOWERS. The only thing that concerns me, where I'm concerned at this point, is the state job.

B. CLINTON. Yeah, I never thought about that, but as long as you say you've just been looking for one, you'd check on it. If they ever ask you if you've talked to me about it, you can say no.

G. FLOWERS. All right, darling. Well, you hang in there. I don't mean to worry you. I just. . . .

B. CLINTON. [garbled] . . . I just want to know these things and . . . if I can help you, you let me know [garbled].

G. FLOWERS. Well, when you can help me is if I decide I want to get the heck out of here.

B. CLINTON. All you need to do is let me know. . . .

G. FLOWERS. Because I don't know . . . I don't know where to turn. I really don't. I mean my contacts have just sort of fizzled in Nashville. It's been a long time and, I don't know—I don't know anybody.

B. CLINTON. [garbled words] . . . I'll help you.

G. FLOWERS. Okay. Well, I'll . . . I'll be back in touch, and, uh, you will let me know if you know anything I need to know about.

B. CLINTON. I will.

G. FLOWERS. Okay? [laughs]

B. CLINTON. Goodbye, baby.

G. FLOWERS. Talk to you later. Bye.

The above tape excerpts only tell part of the story. I don't think an observant listener would have to be Sherlock Holmes to figure out where the truth lies, but the decision is yours.

If you would like to get a fuller sense of my relationship with our forty-second President, I strongly suggest that you purchase the audio tapes and accompanying transcription booklet of the four complete telephone conversations.

References

Chapter 1. Bill Clinton Undressed

Opening quotation is from the song "It's Alright, Ma (I'm Only Bleeding)" by Bob Dylan (copyright renewed 1993, Special Rider Music), which appeared in the Columbia album *Bringing It All Back Home.*

Steve Kroft interview with the Clintons was aired on the CBS Television show *60 Minutes,* January 27, 1992.

Thomas Moore quote is from Thomas Moore, *SoulMates: Honoring the Mysteries of Love and Relationship* (New York: HarperCollins, 1994) p. 11.

Allegations of the president sneaking out of the White House are made in Gary Aldrich, *Unlimited Access: An FBI Agent Inside the Clinton White House* (Washington, D.C.: Regnery Publishing, Inc., 1996) pp. 135-146.

"You have to remember," an old Arkansas friend recalled, "that
    Billy grew up. . . . " was quoted in Roger Morris, *Partners in
    Power: The Clintons and Their America* (New York: Henry Holt,
    1996) p. 151.
Professor Larry Sabato's comments were aired on *Donahue*, January,
    27, 1992, "Tabloid Scandal Hits Democratic Front-Runner."
Godfather quotes are from Mario Puzo, *The Godfather* (Greenwich,
    CT: Fawcett-Crest Books, 1969.) p. 509 and p. 364.
Reports of former Miss Arkansas being threatened were covered in
    Ambrose Evans-Pritchard, "I Was Threatened After Clinton
    Affair," *Sunday Telegraph* (London), January 23, 1994.
Revelations of the Arkansas state troopers are covered in David Brock,
    "Living with the Clintons," the *American Spectator,* January 1994.
"It was not that Clinton had governed and then made his sexual
    forays as part of some scrupulously separate private life. . . . " is
    quoted from Roger Morris, *Partners in Power: The Clintons and
    Their America* (New York: Henry Holt, 1996) p. 444.

Chapter 2. What Did I Get Myself Into?
Opening quotation is from Tony Snow, "Judging Clinton's Honor,"
    Washington Times, January 3, 1994.

Chapter 3. Our First Date
Opening quotation is from Bill Clinton talking about Hillary to
    Gail Sheehy, "What Hillary Wants," *Vanity Fair*, May 1992.

Chapter 4. The Passion Begins
Opening quotation is from the introduction to Thomas Moore,
    SoulMates: Honoring the Mysteries of Love and Relationship (New
    York: HarperCollins, 1994).

Chapter 5. Momma's Boy and Lover Man
Opening quotation is from Ecclesiastes—Song of Solomon 7:10.
Nigel Hamilton's observations on John F. Kennedy's relationship

with his mother are quoted from Nigel Hamilton, *JFK, Reckless Youth* (New York: Random House, 1992) p. 49.

William Blythe's previous marriages are covered in Roger Morris, *Partners in Power: The Clintons and Their America* (New York: Henry Holt, 1996) pp. 20-21.

Bill Clinton's mother is quoted in Virginia Kelley, *Leading with My Heart* (New York: Simon & Schuster, 1994) p. 65.

Young Bill Clinton's confrontation with his stepfather was reported in, among other places, the *Washington Post*, January 26, 1992.

Chapter 6. A Dream That Could Never Come True

Opening quotation is taken from a letter Bill Clinton wrote, dated September 26, 1986 to the Arkansas Right to Life office expressing his opposition to abortion. The letter was reproduced in Floyd G. Brown, *"Slick Willie": Why America Cannot Trust Bill Clinton* (Annapolis, MD: Annapolis-Washington Book Publishers, 1994).

"Theirs was a fortuitous, even extraordinary pairing. . . . " is quoted from Meredith L. Oakley, *On the Make: The Rise of Bill Clinton* (Washington,, D.C.: Regnery Publishing, Inc.) 1994, p. 90.

Chapter 7. Stolen Moments with Mr. Kinky

Opening quotation is from David Letterman, *The Late Show,* July 19, 1996.

Chapter 8. Portrait of a Risk Junkie

Opening quotation is from Joe Klein, "The Politics of Promiscuity," *Newsweek,* May 9, 1994.

Chapter 9. The Long Goodbye

Opening quotation is from "Anonymous," *Primary Colors* (New York: Random House, 1996) p. 63.

Mandy Grunwald's interchange with Ted Koppel took place on *ABC*

News Nightline, "Tabloid Prints New Bill Clinton Infidelity Charge," January 23, 1992.

Grunwald's role in defending Clinton on *Nightline* and her subsequent hiring as media and advertising director for the 1992 campaign is covered in Bob Woodward, *The Agenda: Inside the Clinton White House* (New York: Pocket Books, 1994) p. 26.

The list of Bill Clinton's sexual indiscretions was culled from various sources and summarized in Richard Gooding, "The Clinton Sex Files," *Star*, July 9, 1996.

Joe Klein is quoted from "The Politics of Promiscuity," *Newsweek*, May 9, 1994.

Allegations of President Clinton's trysts with a woman at Washington's Marriott Hotel are cited in Gary Aldrich, *Unlimited Access: An FBI Agent Inside the Clinton White House*, (Washington, D.C.: Regnery Publishing, Inc., 1996) pp. 135–146.